. . .when you need it in writing!®

CORPORATE SECRETARY®

Prepare and maintain your own corporate records without a lawyer.

prepared by
Mario D. German, Esquire
FLORIDA BAR MEMBER

edited by
Sondra Servais

E·Z LEGAL⁽ᴵᴸ⁾ BOOKS

384 South Military Trail, Deerfield Beach, FL 33442
phone: (954) 480-8933 • fax: (954) 480-8906

... when you need it in writing! ®

E-Z Legal Forms, Inc.
384 S. Military Trail
Deerfield Beach FL 33442

Distributed by E-Z Legal Forms, Inc.

Manufactured in the United States of America

3 4 5 6 7 8 9 10

Library of Congress Catalog Card Number: 93-074657

Corporate Secretary
   Compiled by Mario D. German, Esquire
   Sondra Servais, editor.
      p.   cm.
   ISBN 1-56382-304-7: $24.95
I. German, Mario D., compiled by. II. Servais, Sondra, edited by. III.
Title: Corporate Secretary

IMPORTANT FACTS

E-Z Legal Products are designed to provide authoritative and accurate information in regard to the subject matter covered. However, neither this nor any other publication can take the place of an attorney on important legal matters.

Information in this book has been carefully compiled from sources believed to be reliable, but the accuracy of the information is not guaranteed as laws and regulations may change or be subject to differing interpretations.

Why not have your attorney review this book? We encourage it.

PRINTED IN THE UNITED STATES OF AMERICA

E-Z LEGAL FORMS
384 South Military Trail
Deerfield Beach, FL 33442
Tel. (954)-480-8933   Fax (954)-480-8906

About Corporate Secretary...

Corporate Secretary contains all the important and ready-to-complete forms and documents you need to keep proper corporate minutes and records.

Virtually every corporate record keeping form is at your fingertips, giving you the protection you need without the inconvenience or cost of using an attorney for simple corporate matters you can easily handle yourself.

E-Z Legal Forms' *Corporate Secretary* is the ideal way to "get it in writing." What better way is there to legally document your important corporate transactions, avoid troublesome disputes, enforce your legal rights, comply with legal obligations and avoid liability?

Virtually every size and type of corporation can use *Corporate Secretary*. It can be used by both non-profit and profit corporations as well as by "S" corporations and regular "C" corporations. It will be particularly useful to small and mid-sized corporations which require less formal record keeping than larger, publicly owned corporations.

Written by a panel of attorneys and law professors, *Corporate Secretary* is considered safe and effective for use by non-lawyers.

How to Use Corporate Secretary

You can easily and conveniently use *Corporate Secretary* by following these simple instructions.

1 To find the appropriate form, you can check the Table of Contents. Each entry contains a cross-reference to our *Corporate Secretary* software.

2 You may find several forms for the same general purpose, so review and select the form most appropriate for your specific needs.

3 Each form is perforated for easy removal and use. Photocopy and store the original so it can be used again and again.

4 Fully complete each form. Make certain all blanks (name, address, dates, amounts) are filled in. Delete, modify or add provisions as required. Attach a separate addendum if additional terms cannot be easily inserted. All changes or addendums should be initialed by all parties. Verbal terms are generally not enforceable, so make certain your document includes all that was agreed upon.

5 Correspondence forms can be personalized by reproducing on your letterhead.

6 Read the material that precedes each section for a description of each form.

7 The pronoun "it" within a form can properly refer to an individual as well as a business entity.

8 Important correspondence should always be delivered by certified mail, return receipt requested.

9 Use caution and common sense when using E-Z Legal Forms — or any other do-it-yourself legal product. While these forms are generally considered appropriate for self-use, you must nevertheless decide when you should instead seek professional legal advice. You should certainly consult an attorney when:

- You need a complex or important agreement.
- Your transaction involves large amounts of money or expensive property.
- You don't understand how to use a document — or question its adequacy to fully protect you.

Because we cannot be certain that the forms in this book are appropriate to your circumstances — or are being properly used — we cannot assume any liability or responsibility in connection with their use.

Table of Contents

Section One

Section Two

Section Three

Section Four

Section Five

Section Six

Section Seven

Table of Contents (alphabetical)

A – L

M – P

R

S – W

How Corporate Secretary Can Help You

Why good corporate records are essential

No business owner has become wealthy simply because he or she kept good corporate records. Yet, good corporate record keeping is essential for several important reasons.

1. *To protect you legally.*

Generally, when you create a corporation, you create a legal entity separate and distinct from you as an individual. That means the corporation is responsible for its own actions. You are not legally responsible for the acts of the corporation, unless it engages in any criminal activity. That's why it's important for you to document all of the actions of the corporation. Without well-maintained corporate records, the courts may disregard your corporate status and allow creditors to sue you personally for debts of the business. This is called *piercing the corporate veil*. This means the courts can conclude that because the corporation did not accept its responsibilities and document its transactions, it is only a *sham*, or mere alter-ego of its owners.

This problem occurs more often than you may think. Quite often an owner of a business cannot prove that the corporation acted for its own purposes rather than that of the owner personally. This inevitably leads to personal as well as corporate liability for the business debts.

If your corporation has multiple stockholders, the need for detailed corporate records becomes even more critical. Any one stockholder may quite easily challenge the authority for a transaction. Only complete and accurate resolutions can demonstrate that the action was properly authorized by the stockholders and/or the directors.

A corporation can encounter many additional legal problems. Where transactions require director or stockholder approval, then a detailed record of the transaction as discussed and/or voted at a directors' or stockholders' meeting may resolve the dispute in your favor.

As an officer or director of a large corporation, you must particularly insist upon accurate minutes so you can prove your actions at these meetings and also show matters you voted against. Because lawsuits against directors are common, you must be able to defend your every action on behalf of the corporation. This is possible only with written proof, and that means good corporate records.

2.   *To gain important tax benefits.*

The IRS is particularly demanding when it comes to corporate records. Have the corporate benefits you enjoy been properly voted? Have loans between you and your corporation been authorized in writing? Did you hold the required meetings to decide upon becoming an "S" Corporation or to change your corporation's fiscal year? Do you have resolutions authorizing your own salary?

The IRS will inspect your corporate minute book and without written documents to support the actions of the corporation, it may disallow any tax benefits resulting from those actions. This can produce a large tax liability—only because you failed to take the few moments necessary to keep up-to-date corporate minutes.

Don't you lose your valuable tax benefits. Make good corporate record keeping an essential part of your tax schedule.

The corporate organization

Corporate Secretary is the perfect way to keep good records of all corporate transactions... quickly, efficiently, inexpensively and professionally.

You can incorporate in any state, Puerto Rico or the District of Columbia, and much has been said about incorporating in corporate-friendly states like Delaware or Nevada. However, small corporations are advised to incorporate in the state where they are located and do business. If you do business across state lines, you may have to qualify as a "foreign corporation" in states other than your own. But incorporating in the state where you are located makes the most sense.

Once you have decided where to incorporate, a great deal of information about how to set up your corporation free or for minimal fees can be obtained from the Secretary of State of that state. Additionally, most states provide their own specific Certificate (or Articles) of Incorporation. We also provide a generic Articles of Incorporation in this book, which may meet your state's requirements.

Before filling out any incorporation records, contact your secretary of state. A listing of the addresses and telephone numbers is found at the end of this book.

Any corporation, whether large or small, conducts its affairs through three different groups:

- officers
- directors
- stockholders

Corporations, of course, also function through employees who carry out the day-to-day mandates of the officers. In most states one person may occupy all positions in the corporation (president, treasurer and secretary) and be its sole stockholder and director. Let's examine more closely the functions of each group.

Officers

Every corporation must have three officers:

- President
- Treasurer
- Secretary (or clerk)

As stated, one person may generally serve in all three capacities, although the person's responsibility and authority necessarily changes through the different officerships the person assumes.

In addition to these statutory officerships, there may be vice presidents and/or assistant secretaries or clerks.

In each case, the authority of each officer is spelled out in the corporate bylaws and may be further defined by an employment contract or job description.

The president has the overall executive responsibility for the management of the corporation and is directly responsible for carrying out the orders of the board. The president may be elected by the board or by the stockholders. The bylaws prescribe this procedure.

The treasurer has a narrower role. The treasurer is the chief financial officer of the corporation and is responsible for controlling and recording its finances. Actual fiscal policy of the corporation may rest with the Board of Directors and be largely controlled by the president on a day-to-day basis.

The corporate secretary is responsible for maintaining the corporate records. This product derives its name *Corporate Secretary* from this office because it handles the role of keeping corporate records so effectively.

Directors

The Board of Directors is the overall management body for the corporation. The board is responsible for establishing all business policies and for approving major contracts and undertakings. The board may also elect the president. Ordinary business practices of the corporation are carried out by the officers—and employees—under the directives and supervision of the directors.

The directors must act collectively for their votes and decisions to be valid. That's why directors act at a Board of Directors meeting. This, however, requires certain formalities. One is that the directors must be notified of a forthcoming meeting in a prescribed manner, although this can be waived or provided for in the corporation's Articles of Incorporation or Bylaws. For a directors' meeting to be valid, there must also be a quorum of directors present. A quorum is usually a majority of the directors then serving on the board; however, the bylaws may specify another minimum number or percentage.

Boards meet on a regular basis (monthly or quarterly), but in no case less than annually. These are the *regular* meetings. Boards may also call *special* meetings for matters that may arise between regular meetings. In addition, boards may call a special shareholders' meeting by adopting a resolution stating where and when the meeting is to be held and what business is to be transacted.

The first meeting of the Board of Directors is important because the bylaws, the corporate seal, stock certificates and record books are adopted. If your corporation is an existing one, use the resolutions contained in this book as a checklist to insure your corporation has satisfied all legal requirements.

Board members, like officers, have a fiduciary duty to act in the best interests of the corporation and cannot put their own interests ahead of the corporation's. The board must also act prudently and not negligently manage the affairs of the corporation. Finally, the board must make certain that it properly exercises its authority in managing the corporation and does not abrogate its responsibilities to others.

This means that the board must be very careful to document that each board action was reasonable, lawful and in the best interests of the corporation. This is particularly true with matters involving compensation, dividends and dealings involving officers, directors and stockholders. The record—or minutes of the meeting—must include the arguments or statements to support the action and why it was proper.

Stockholders

Since the stockholders own the corporation, the officers and directors must ultimately serve their interests.

Still, this does not mean that stockholders are powerless concerning the affairs of their corporation. The rights of the stockholders are governed by the bylaws of the corporation as well as by prevailing state laws.

Generally, the stockholders vote on the following matters:

1. Appointment of the president

2.   Election of the Board of Directors

3.   Major changes in the basic organization of the corporation. This may include:

- change of name or address
- change in the nature of business
- change in bylaws
- change in type and number of shares of stock issued
- change in size or composition of board
- encumbering corporate assets
- dissolution or winding down of the corporation
- selling, consolidating or merging the corporation.

Stockholders, like directors, cannot act unilaterally. They must act either at a regular stockholders' meeting (ordinarily held annually after the end of the fiscal year) or at a special meeting of the stockholders (ordinarily called at the request of the board).

There must be notice of the meeting and notice of the agenda (items to be discussed and voted upon). Most states require 10 days' notice and not more than 50 or 60 days' notice be provided. You can specify a time period in the corporation's Articles of Incorporation. Waivers of notice are allowed if the Board fails to notify stockholders of the meeting or an emergency prevents adequate notice.

Stockholders may vote in person or vote by proxy, which means having another person vote in the stockholder's place. It is important to remember that shareholders vote their shares and it is the number of shares—not the number of shareholders—that decide the vote.

As with directors, there must also be a complete and accurate record—or minutes—of a stockholders' meeting.

Some states allow certain actions, e.g., amending the Articles of Incorporation, to be taken without holding a stockholders' meeting if (1) the corporation obtains a written consent to the action from the stockholders, and (2) the written consent states what action the stockholders have consented to. Check with your state to find out how many stockholders must sign a consent for it to be valid.

Occasionally, there will be a combined meeting of stockholders and directors. This is perfectly permissible, however, you still need complete minutes of meetings.

Running your corporation

Resolutions record the major decisions taken by the corporation's stockholders or Board of Directors. While not always required, it is a good idea to record your actions in the form of resolutions because they show outsiders that the actions were taken by and on behalf of the corporation. Some resolutions are passed only by the stockholders; others, only by the Board of Directors. Some must be passed by both bodies.

Any changes to the corporation's Articles of Incorporation or Bylaws must be approved by both the stockholders and directors. Amendments to the Articles of Incorporation must then be filed with the Secretary of State in the state of incorporation for the amendments to become effective. Some states also require corporations to file a notarized affidavit, which verifies the number of outstanding shares at the time of the vote. Stockholders must also vote to dissolve the corporation or to file for bankruptcy or reorganization.

Resolutions adopted by the Board of Directors that generally do not require stockholder approval involve everyday operations of the corporation, including leasing, major purchases, hiring, banking, borrowing, investing, paying of dividends, salaries and bonuses, providing benefits for employees and changing the corporate status, such as obtaining "S" status.

As a general rule all records, resolutions and minutes of your coporation should be kept in your corporate minute book for a period of no less than six years. This is a good idea because sometimes a stockholder will want to inspect the corporate books and records to insure the corporation is being run in its best interests. We recommend that your corporation retain these records for a longer period should anyone ever challenge the actions of the Board.

Corporate Secretary provides you with the tools necessary to meet all legal requirements. If properly utilized, it will provide all of the tax benefits and liability protection that a corporation affords you.

The following page contains a helpful checklist which will aid you in properly using and maintaining a sound record system for your corporation.

Do you keep good corporate records?

Ask yourself these questions:

1 Are board and stockholder meetings regularly scheduled in advance and adequate in both number and time to cover all business properly?

2 Are meeting agendas and the necessary background information provided well in advance of the meeting?

3 Do directors have reasonable opportunity to add agenda items?

4 Is each agenda item fully acted upon or advanced to a future meeting?

5 Is there adequate time to discuss each agenda item, and is each director and/or stockholder afforded a reasonable opportunity to discuss the issue?

6 Are minutes of each meeting accurately recorded? Do the minutes reflect how each director voted on each issue?

7 Does the board meet with and/or receive direct reports from each committee, legal counsel, accountants, and other outside advisors? Are these reports included with the minutes?

8 Are the minutes of committee and/or board meetings reviewed at subsequent meetings? Are they amended or corrected for clarity and accuracy? Are the dissents to the minutes duly recorded?

9 Do board meetings adequately cover substantive policy issues involving the corporation rather than only trivia or administrative detail?

10 Does the board chairperson effectively conduct board meetings?

Section Two
Corporate Organization

Form A201   Verifies the number of shares of stock owned by each stockholder of the corporation.

Form A202   Contains standard articles of organization used to file with the state to charter the corporation. Certain states require use of their own form. Check with your Secretary of State before filing.

Form B201   Contains the bylaws of the corporation. The bylaws are the internal rules for conducting the affairs of the corporation.

Form C201   Is used to change the corporate structure or organization.

Form C202   Is a certificate of dissolution for the corporation.

Form I201   Acknowledges the incumbent officers of the corporation.

Form N201   Is a notice to an officer of removal from the Board of Directors.

Form R201   Accepts director's resignation.

Form R202   Accepts an officer's resignation.

Form R203   Adopts amendment to Articles of Incorporation.

Form R204   Authorizes the adoption of a corporate seal.

Form R205   Is the resolution authorizing the amendment to the Articles of Incorporation.

Form R206   Specifically authorizes an amendment or change to the bylaws.

Form R207   Authorizes amendment to bylaws with shareholder approval.

Form R208   Authorizes appointment of an officer or director.

Form R209   Allows the directors complete or blanket authority to amend bylaws.

Form R210   Is a stockholder resolution increasing the number of authorized shares.

Form R211   Authorizes change in corporate address.

Form R212   Authorizes change of the corporate name.

Form R213   Authorizes change in corporate fiscal year.

Form R214   Is a board resolution increasing the number of authorized shares.

Form R215   Authorizes the dissolution of the corporation and calls for shareholder approval.

Form R216   Extends appointment of an officer or director.

Form R217   Authorizes the filling of a vacancy on the board.

Form R218   Authorizes the corporation to elect subchapter "S" tax status.

Form R219   Authorizes the removal of an officer or director.

Form R220   Requests the resignation of an officer.

Form R221   Authorizes the termination of foreign corporation status.

Form R222   Authorizes the termination of "S" status and reversion to regular "C" corporation status.

AFFIDAVIT VERIFYING NUMBER OF SHARES

AFFIDAVIT OF SECRETARY OF

_____

State of
County of

, being duly sworn, deposes and says:

1. That I am the Secretary of _____, a Corporation duly created, organized, and existing under and by virtue of the laws of the State of _____ .

2. That I am the custodian of the stock book of the said

3. That the total number of shares of the capital stock of the said Corporation issued and outstanding on _____ , 19 , is shares, and that the persons whose signatures are affixed to the foregoing consent constitute the holders of more than a majority of the said capital stock so issued and outstanding.

_____
Secretary

State of
County of

On _____ before me, personally appeared _____ ,

who personally known to me (or proved to me on the basis of satisfactory evidence) to be the person(s) whose name(s) is/are subscribed to the within instrument and acknowledged to me that he/she/they executed the same in his/her/their authorized capacity(ies), and that by his/her/their signature(s) on the instrument the person(s), or the entity upon behalf of which the person(s) acted, executed the instrument.
WITNESS my hand and official seal.

Signature_____

My commission expires:

Affiant _____Known _____Produced ID

Type of ID _____

(Seal)

Articles of Incorporation

We, the undersigned, as proper persons acting as incorporators of a corporation under the laws of the state of _____, adopt the following articles of incorporation:

FIRST   The name of the corporation is:_____.

SECOND   The period of its duration is:_____.

THIRD   The purpose of the corporation is:_____

_____.

FOURTH   The aggregate number of authorized shares is:_____.

FIFTH   The corporation will not commence business until at least _____

_____ dollars have been received by it as consideration

for the issuance of shares.

SIXTH   Cumulative voting of shares of stock [is] [is not] authorized.

SEVENTH Provisions limiting or denying to shareholders the pre-emptive right to

acquire additional or treasury shares of the corporation are:

_____

_____.

EIGHTH   Provisions for regulating of the internal affairs of the corporation are:

_____

_____.

NINTH   The address of the initial registered office of the corporation is:

_____

and the name of its initial registered agent at such address is:

_____.

TENTH   Address of the principal place of business is:_____

_____.

ELEVENTH The number of directors constituting the initial board of directors of the corporation is_____, and the names and address of the persons who are to serve as directors until the first annual meeting of shareholders or until their successors are elected and shall qualify are:

Name   Address

_____   _____

_____   _____

_____   _____

TWELFTH   The name and address of each incorporator is:

Name   Address

_____   _____

_____   _____

_____   _____

Date

BYLAWS
of

_____

adopted_____

BYLAWS
OF

_____

ARTICLE I: OFFICES

The principal office of the Corporation in the State of

shall be located in   , County of   . The

Corporation may have such other offices, either within or without the State of

, as the Board of Directors may designate or as the business of the Corporation may

require from time to time.

ARTICLE II: SHAREHOLDERS

SECTION 1. Annual Meeting. The annual meeting of the shareholders shall

be held on the   day in the month of   in each year, beginning with

the year 19   , at the hour of   .m., for the purpose of electing Directors and for

the transaction of such other business as may come before the meeting. If the day fixed for

the annual meeting shall be a legal holiday in the State of   , such

meeting shall be held on the next succeeding business day. If the election of Directors shall

not be held on the day designated herein for any annual meeting of the shareholders, or at

any adjournment thereof, the Board of Directors shall cause the election to be held at a

special meeting of the shareholders as soon thereafter as conveniently may be.

SECTION 2. Special Meetings. Special meetings of the shareholders, for any

purpose or purposes, unless otherwise prescribed by statute, may be called by the

President or by the Board of Directors, and shall be called by the President at the request of the holders of not less than   percent (%) of all the outstanding shares of the Corporation entitled to vote at the meeting.

SECTION 3. Place of Meeting. The Board of Directors may designate any place, either within or without the State of   , unless otherwise prescribed by statute, as the place of meeting for any annual meeting or for any special meeting. A waiver of notice signed by all shareholders entitled to vote at a meeting may designate any place, either within or without the State of   , unless otherwise prescribed by statute, as the place for the holding of such meeting. If no designation is made, the place of meeting shall be the principal office of the Corporation.

SECTION 4. Notice of Meeting. Written notice stating the place, day and hour of the meeting and, in case of a special meeting, the purpose or purposes for which the meeting is called, shall unless otherwise prescribed by statute, be delivered not less than (   )   nor more than (   )   days before the date of the meeting, to each shareholder of record entitled to vote at such meeting. If mailed, such notice shall be deemed to be delivered when deposited in the United States Mail, addressed to the shareholder at his address as it appears on the stock transfer books of the Corporation, with postage thereon prepaid.

SECTION 5. Closing of Transfer Books or Fixing of Record. For the purpose of determining shareholders entitled to notice of or to vote at any meeting of shareholders or any adjournment thereof, or shareholders entitled to receive payment of any dividend, or in order to make a determination of shareholders for any other proper purpose, the Board of Directors of the Corporation may provide that the stock transfer books shall be closed for a stated period, but not to exceed in any case fifty (50) days. If the stock transfer books shall be closed for the purpose of determining shareholders entitled to notice of or to vote at a meeting of shareholders, such books shall be closed for at least ( ) days immediately preceding such meeting. In lieu of closing the stock transfer books, the Board of Directors may fix in advance a date as the record date for any such determination of shareholders, such date in any case to be not more than ( ) days and, in case of a meeting of shareholders, not less than ( ) days, prior to the date on which the particular action requiring such determination of shareholders is to be taken. If the stock transfer books are not closed and no record date is fixed for the determination of shareholders entitled to notice of or to vote at a meeting of shareholders, or shareholders entitled to receive payment of a dividend, the date on which notice of the meeting is mailed or the date on which the resolution of the Board of Directors declaring such dividend is adopted, as the case may be, shall be the record date for such determination of shareholders. When a determination of shareholders entitled to vote at any meeting of shareholders has been made as provided in this section, such determination shall apply to any adjournment thereof.

SECTION 6. Voting Lists. The officer or agent having charge of the stock transfer books for shares of the corporation shall make a complete list of the shareholders entitled to vote at each meeting of shareholders or any adjournment thereof, arranged in alphabetical order, with the address of and the number of shares held by each. Such list shall be produced and kept open at the time and place of the meeting and shall be subject to the inspection of any shareholder during the whole time of the meeting for the purposes thereof.

SECTION 7. Quorum. A majority of the outstanding shares of the Corporation entitled to vote, represented in person or by proxy, shall constitute a quorum at a meeting of shareholders. If less than a majority of the outstanding shares are represented at a meeting, a majority of the shares so represented may adjourn the meeting from time to time without further notice. At such adjourned meeting at which a quorum shall be present or represented, any business may be transacted which might have been transacted at the meeting as originally noticed. The shareholders present at a duly organized meeting may continue to transact business until adjournment, notwithstanding the withdrawal of enough shareholders to leave less than a quorum.

SECTION 8. Proxies. At all meetings of shareholders, a shareholder may vote in person or by proxy executed in writing by the shareholder or by his or her duly authorized attorney-in-fact. Such proxy shall be filed with the secretary of the Corporation before or at the time of the meeting. A meeting of the Board of Directors may be had by means of a telephone conference or similar communications equipment by which all persons participating in the meeting can hear each other, and participation in a meeting under such circumstances shall constitute presence at the meeting.

SECTION 9. Voting of Shares. Each outstanding share entitled to vote shall be entitled to one vote upon each matter submitted to a vote at a meeting of shareholders.

SECTION 10. Voting of Shares by Certain Holders. Shares standing in the name of another corporation may be voted by such officer, agent or proxy as the Bylaws of such corporation may prescribe or, in the absence of such provision, as the Board of Directors of such corporation may determine.

Shares held by an administrator, executor, guardian or conservator may be voted by him either in person or by proxy, without a transfer of such shares into his name. Shares standing in the name of a trustee may be voted by him, either in person or by proxy, but no trustee shall be entitled to vote shares held by him without a transfer of such shares into his name.

Shares standing in the name of a receiver may be voted by such receiver, and shares held by or under the control of a receiver may be voted by such receiver without the transfer thereof into his name, if authority to do so be contained in an appropriate order of the court by which such receiver was appointed.

A shareholder whose shares are pledged shall be entitled to vote such shares until the shares have been transferred into the name of the pledgee, and thereafter the pledgee shall be entitled to vote the shares so transferred.

Shares of its own stock belonging to the Corporation shall not be voted directly or indirectly, at any meeting, and shall not be counted in determining the total number of outstanding shares at any given time.

SECTION 11. Informal Action by Shareholders. Unless otherwise provided by law, any action required to be taken at a meeting of the shareholders, or any other action which may be taken at a meeting of the shareholders, may be taken without a meeting if a consent in writing, setting forth the action so taken, shall be signed by all of the shareholders entitled to vote with respect to the subject matter thereof.

ARTICLE III: BOARD OF DIRECTORS

SECTION 1. General Powers. The business and affairs of the Corporation shall be managed by its Board of Directors.

SECTION 2. Number, Tenure and Qualifications. The number of directors of the Corporation shall be fixed by the Board of Directors, but in no event shall be less than (   ). Each director shall hold office until the next annual meeting of shareholders and until his successor shall have been elected and qualified.

SECTION 3. Regular Meetings. A regular meeting of the Board of Directors shall be held without other notice than this Bylaw immediately after, and at the same place as, the annual meeting of shareholders. The Board of Directors may provide, by resolution, the time and place for the holding of additional regular meetings without notice other than such resolution.

SECTION 4. Special Meetings. Special meetings of the Board of Directors may be called by or at the request of the President or any two directors. The person or persons authorized to call special meetings of the Board of Directors may fix the place for holding any special meeting of the Board of Directors called by them.

SECTION 5. Notice. Notice of any special meeting shall be given at least one (1) day previous thereto by written notice delivered personally or mailed to each director at his business address, or by telegram. If mailed, such notice shall be deemed to be delivered when deposited in the United States Mail so addressed, with postage thereon prepaid. If notice be given by telegram, such notice shall be deemed to be delivered when the telegram is delivered to the telegraph company. Any directors may waive notice of any meeting. The attendance of a director at a meeting shall constitute a waiver of notice of such meeting, except where a director attends a meeting for the express purpose of objecting to the transaction of any business because the meeting is not lawfully called or convened.

SECTION 6. Quorum. A majority of the number of directors fixed by Section 2 of this Article III shall constitute a quorum for the transaction of business at any meeting of the Board of Directors, but if less than such majority is present at a meeting, a majority of the directors present may adjourn the meeting from time to time without further notice.

SECTION 7. Manner of Acting. The act of the majority of the directors present at a meeting at which a quorum is present shall be the act of the Board of Directors.

SECTION 8. Action Without a Meeting. Any action that may be taken by the Board of Directors at a meeting may be taken without a meeting if a consent in writing, setting forth the action so to be taken, shall be signed before such action by all of the directors.

SECTION 9. Vacancies. Any vacancy occurring in the Board of Directors may be filled by the affirmative vote of a majority of the remaining directors though less than a quorum of the Board of Directors, unless otherwise provided by law. A director elected to fill a vacancy shall be elected for the unexpired term of his predecessor in office. Any directorship to be filled by reason of an increase in the number of directors may be filled by election by the Board of Directors for a term of office continuing only until the next election of directors by the shareholders.

SECTION 10. Compensation. By resolution of the Board of Directors, each director may be paid his expenses, if any, of attendance at each meeting of the Board of Directors, and may be paid a stated salary as a director or a fixed sum for attendance at each meeting of the Board of Directors or both. No such payment shall preclude any director from serving the Corporation in any other capacity and receiving compensation thereof.

SECTION 11. Presumption of Assent. A director of the Corporation who is present at a meeting of the Board of Directors at which action on any corporate matter is taken shall be presumed to have assented to the action taken unless his dissent shall be entered in the minutes of the meeting or unless he shall file his written dissent to such action with the person acting as the Secretary of the meeting before the adjournment thereof, or shall forward such dissent by registered mail to the Secretary of the Corporation immediately after the adjournment of the meeting. Such right to dissent shall not apply to a director who voted in favor of such action.

ARTICLE IV: OFFICERS

SECTION 1. Number. The officers of the Corporation shall be a President, one or more Vice Presidents, a Secretary and a Treasurer, each of whom shall be elected by the Board of Directors. Such other officers and assistant officers as may be deemed necessary may be elected or appointed by the Board of Directors, including a Chairman of the Board. In its discretion, the Board of Directors may leave unfilled for any such period as it may determine any office except those of President and Secretary. Any two or more offices may be held by the same person, except for the offices of President and Secretary which may not be held by the same person. Officers may be directors or shareholders of the Corporation.

SECTION 2. Election and Term of Office. The officers of the Corporation to be elected by the Board of Directors shall be elected annually by the Board of Directors at the first meeting of the Board of Directors held after each annual meeting of the shareholders. If the election of officers shall not be held at such meeting, such election shall be held as soon thereafter as conveniently may be. Each officer shall hold office until his successor shall have been duly elected and shall have qualified, or until his death, or until he shall resign or shall have been removed in the manner hereinafter provided.

SECTION 3. Removal. Any officer or agent may be removed by the Board of Directors whenever, in its judgment, the best interests of the Corporation will be served thereby, but such removal shall be without prejudice to the contract rights, if any, of the person so removed. Election or appointment of an officer or agent shall not of itself create contract rights, and such appointment shall be terminable at will.

SECTION 4. Vacancies. A vacancy in any office because of death, resignation, removal, disqualification or otherwise, may be filled by the Board of Directors for the unexpired portion of the term.

SECTION 5. President. The President shall be the principal executive officer of the Corporation and, subject to the control of the Board of Directors, shall in general supervise and control all of the business and affairs of the Corporation. He shall, when present, preside at all meetings of the shareholders and of the Board of Directors, unless there is a Chairman of the Board, in which case the Chairman shall preside. He may sign, with the Secretary or any other proper officer of the Corporation thereunto authorized by the Board of Directors, certificates for shares of the Corporation, any deeds, mortgages, bonds, contracts, or other instruments which the Board of Directors has authorized to be executed, except in cases where the signing and execution thereof shall be expressly delegated by the Board of Directors or by these Bylaws to some other officer or agent of the Corporation, or shall be required by law to be otherwise signed or executed; and in general shall perform all duties incident to the office of President and such other duties as may be prescribed by the Board of Directors from time to time.

SECTION 6. Vice President. In the absence of the president or in event of his death, inability or refusal to act, the Vice President shall perform the duties of the President, and when so acting, shall have all the powers of and be subject to all the restrictions upon the President. The Vice President shall perform such other duties as from time to time may be assigned to him by the President or by the Board of Directors. If there is more than one Vice President, each Vice President shall succeed to the duties of the President in order of rank as determined by the Board of Directors. If no such rank has been determined, then each Vice President shall succeed to the duties of the President in order of date of election, the earliest date having the first rank.

SECTION 7. Secretary. The Secretary shall: (a) keep the minutes of the proceedings of the shareholders and of the Board of Directors in one or more minute books provided for that purpose; (b) see that all notices are duly given in accordance with the provisions of these Bylaws or as required by law; (c) be custodian of the corporate records and of the seal of the Corporation and see that the seal of the Corporation is affixed to all documents, the execution of which on behalf of the Corporation under its seal is duly authorized; (d) keep a register of the post office address of each shareholder which shall be furnished to the Secretary by such shareholder; (e) sign with the President certificates for shares of the Corporation, the issuance of which shall have been authorized by resolution of the Board of Directors; (f) have general charge of the stock transfer books of the Corporation; and (g) in general perform all duties incident to the office of the Secretary and such other duties as from time to time may be assigned to him by the President or by the Board of Directors.

SECTION 8. Treasurer. The Treasurer shall: (a) have charge and custody of and be responsible for all funds and securities of the Corporation; (b) receive and give receipts for moneys due and payable to the Corporation from any source whatsoever, and deposit all such moneys in the name of the Corporation in such banks, trust companies or other depositories as shall be selected in accordance with the provisions of Article VI of these Bylaws; and (c) in general perform all of the duties incident to the office of Treasurer and such other duties as from time to time may be assigned to him by the President or by the Board of Directors. If required by the Board of Directors, the Treasurer shall give a bond for the faithful discharge of his duties in such sum and with such sureties as the Board of Directors shall determine.

SECTION 9. Salaries. The salaries of the officers shall be fixed from time to time by the Board of Directors, and no officer shall be prevented from receiving such salary by reason of the fact that he is also a director of the Corporation.

ARTICLE V: INDEMNITY

The Corporation shall indemnify its directors, officers and employees as follows:

(a) Every director, officer, or employee of the Corporation shall be indemnified by the Corporation against all expenses and liabilities, including counsel fees, reasonably incurred by or imposed upon him in connection with any proceeding to which he may become involved, by reason of his being or having been a director, officer, employee or agent of the Corporation or is or was serving at the request of the Corporation as a director, officer, employee or agent of the corporation, partnership, joint venture, trust or enterprise, or any settlement thereof, whether or not he is a director, officer, employee or agent at the time such expenses are incurred, except in such cases wherein the director, officer, or employee is adjudged guilty of willful misfeasance or malfeasance in the performance of his duties; provided that in the event of a settlement the indemnification herein shall apply only when the Board of Directors approves such settlement and reimbursement as being for the best interests of the Corporation.

(b) The Corporation shall provide to any person who is or was a director, officer, employee, or agent of the Corporation or is or was serving at the request of the Corporation as a director, officer, employee or agent of the corporation, partnership, joint venture, trust or enterprise, the indemnity against expenses of suit, litigation or other proceedings which is specifically permissible under applicable law.

(c) The Board of Directors may, in its discretion, direct the purchase of liability insurance by way of implementing the provisions of this Article V.

ARTICLE VI: CONTRACTS, LOANS, CHECKS AND DEPOSITS

SECTION 1. Contracts. The Board of Directors may authorize any officer or officers, agent or agents, to enter into any contract or execute and deliver any instrument in the name of and on behalf of the Corporation, and such authority may be general or confined to specific instances.

SECTION 2. Loans. No loans shall be contracted on behalf of the Corporation and no evidences of indebtedness shall be issued in its name unless authorized by a resolution of the Board of Directors. Such authority may be general or confined to specific instances.

SECTION 3. Checks, Drafts, etc. All checks, drafts or other orders for the payment of money, notes or other evidences of indebtedness issued in the name of the Corporation, shall be signed by such officer or officers, agent or agents of the Corporation and in such manner as shall from time to time be determined by resolution of the Board of Directors.

SECTION 4. Deposits. All funds of the Corporation not otherwise employed shall be deposited from time to time to the credit of the Corporation in such banks, trust companies or other depositories as the Board of Directors may select.

ARTICLE VII
CERTIFICATES FOR SHARES AND THEIR TRANSFER

SECTION 1. Certificates for Shares. Certificates representing shares of the Corporation shall be in such form as shall be determined by the Board of Directors. Such certificates shall be signed by the President and by the Secretary or by such other officers authorized by law and by the Board of Directors so to do, and sealed with the corporate seal. All certificates for shares shall be consecutively numbered or otherwise identified. The name and address of the person to whom the shares represented thereby are issued, with the number of shares and date of issue, shall be entered on the stock transfer books of the Corporation. All certificates surrendered to the Corporation for transfer shall be cancelled and no new certificate shall be issued until the former certificate for a like number of shares shall have been surrendered and cancelled, except that in case of a lost, destroyed or mutilated certificate a new one may be issued therefore upon such terms and indemnity to the Corporation as the Board of Directors may prescribe.

SECTION 2. Transfer of Shares. Transfer of shares of the Corporation shall be made only on the stock transfer books of the Corporation by the holder of record thereof or by his legal representative, who shall furnish proper evidence of authority to transfer, or by his attorney thereunto authorized by power of attorney duly executed and filed with the Secretary of the Corporation, and on surrender for cancellation of the certificate for such shares. The person in whose name shares stand on the books of the Corporation shall be deemed by the Corporation to be the owner thereof for all purposes. Provided, however, that upon any action undertaken by the shareholders to elect S Corporation status pursuant to Section 1362 of the Internal Revenue Code and upon any shareholders agreement thereto restricting the transfer of said shares so as to disqualify said S Corporation status, said restriction on transfer shall be made a part of the Bylaws so long as said agreement is in force and effect.

ARTICLE VIII: FISCAL YEAR

The fiscal year of the Corporation shall begin on the   day of   and end on the   day of   of each year.

ARTICLE IX: DIVIDENDS

The Board of Directors may from time to time declare, and the Corporation may pay, dividends on its outstanding shares in the manner and upon the terms and conditions provided by law and its Articles of Incorporation.

ARTICLE X: CORPORATE SEAL

The Board of Directors shall provide a corporate seal which shall be circular in form and shall have inscribed thereon the name of the Corporation and the state of incorporation and the words, *Corporate Seal*.

ARTICLE XI: WAIVER OF NOTICE

Unless otherwise provided by law, whenever any notice is required to be given to any shareholder or director of the Corporation under the provisions of these Bylaws or under the provisions of the Articles of Incorporation or under the provisions of the applicable Business Corporation Act, a waiver thereof in writing, signed by the person or persons entitled to such notice, whether before or after the time stated therein, shall be deemed equivalent to the giving of such notice.

ARTICLE XII: AMENDMENTS

These Bylaws may be altered, amended or repealed and new Bylaws may be adopted by the Board of Directors at any regular or special meeting of the Board of Directors.

The above Bylaws are certified to have been adopted by the Board of Directors of the Corporation on the   day of   , 19   .

_____
Secretary

CERTIFICATE OF AMENDMENT

_____

, a corporation of the State of

whose registered office is located at

, certifies pursuant to the provisions of

, that at a meeting of the stockholders of said corporation called for the purpose of

amending the Articles of Incorporation, and held on   , 19   , it was resolved

by the vote of the holders of an appropriate majority of the shares of each class entitled to

vote that ARTICLE   of the Articles of Incorporation is amended to read as

follows:

ARTICLE

Signed on

By_____
President

_____
Secretary

CERTIFICATE OF DISSOLUTION

_____

WE, the President and Secretary of   , in accordance
with the requirements of the Corporation Law of the State of   and for
purposes of obtaining the dissolution of said Corporation, as provided by said Law,

DO HEREBY CERTIFY AS FOLLOWS:

The registered office of   in the State of
          is at   =   .

The agent in charge thereof, upon whom process against this Corporation may be
served, is   ,   ,

The dissolution of said   has been duly authorized
under the provisions of Section   of Corporation Law of the State of
          .

The following are the names and residences of all the directors of the said Corporation:

NAME   ADDRESS

Dated: _____
                                President

                                _____
                                Secretary

INCUMBENCY CERTIFICATE

I, _____ , Secretary of _____ ,

do hereby affirm and verify that the duly constituted officers of the Corporation as of

_____ , 19____ , are:

_____ , President

_____ , Vice President

_____ , Treasurer

_____ , Secretary

A True Record:

Attest:

_____
Secretary

State of

County of

On _____ before me, _____ ,
personally appeared

who personally known to me (or proved to me on the basis of satisfactory evidence) to be
the person(s) whose name(s) is/are subscribed to the within instrument and acknowledged
to me that he/she/they executed the same in his/her/their authorized capacity(ies), and
that by his/her/their signature(s) on the instrument the person(s), or the entity upon
behalf of which the person(s) acted, executed the instrument.
WITNESS my hand and official seal.

Signature_____

My commission expires: _____

Affiant _____ Known _____ Produced ID
Type of ID _____

(Seal)

NOTICE TO OFFICER OF REMOVAL FROM BOARD

Date:

To:

PLEASE TAKE NOTICE that, pursuant to Article   , Section   of the Bylaws of this Corporation, the Board of Directors did, at a meeting held on   ,

19   , adopt a resolution removing you forthwith from the office of director, a copy of which resolution is annexed hereto and the original of which is on file in the principal office of the Corporation.

_____
Secretary

RESOLUTION:
ACCEPT DIRECTOR'S RESIGNATION

RESOLVED, that the resignation of   as a member of the

Board of Directors of the Corporation as evidenced by a resignation letter to the

Corporation, dated   , 19   , is hereby accepted, and the Secretary of

the Corporation is hereby instructed to notify   of the Board's

acceptance.

The undersigned hereby certifies that he/she is the duly elected and qualified Secretary

and the custodian of the books and records and seal of   ,

a corporation duly formed pursuant to the laws of the State of   ,

and that the foregoing is a true record of a resolution duly adopted at a meeting of the

Board of Directors, and that said meeting was held in accordance with state law and the

Bylaws of the above-named Corporation on   , 19   , and that said

resolution is now in full force and effect without modification or rescission.

IN WITNESS WHEREOF, I have executed my name as Secretary and have hereunto

affixed the corporate seal of the above-named Corporation this   day of   ,

19   .

A True Record.

Attest.

_____
Secretary

RESOLUTION:
ACCEPT OFFICER'S RESIGNATION

RESOLVED, that the resignation of   , as

of the Corporation as evidenced by a resignation letter to the

Corporation dated   , 19   , is hereby accepted, and the Secretary of

the Corporation is hereby instructed to notify   of the

acceptance of said resignation and to further notify such public offices as are necessary.

The undersigned hereby certifies that he/she is the duly elected and qualified Secretary

and the custodian of the books and records and seal of   ,

a corporation duly formed pursuant to the laws of the State of   ,

and that the foregoing is a true record of a resolution duly adopted at a meeting of the

Board of Directors, and that said meeting was held in accordance with state law and the

Bylaws of the above-named Corporation on   , 19   , and that said

resolution is now in full force and effect without modification or rescission.

IN WITNESS WHEREOF, I have executed my name as Secretary and have hereunto

affixed the corporate seal of the above-named Corporation this   day of   ,

19   .

A True Record.

Attest.

_____
Secretary

RESOLUTION:
ADOPT AMENDMENT TO ARTICLES

RESOLVED, to amend the Articles of Incorporation in accordance with the proposed amendment as set forth on annexed document, and to duly file necessary notices of amendment with the Division of Corporations.

The undersigned hereby certifies that he/she is the duly elected and qualified Secretary and the custodian of the books and records and seal of

a corporation duly formed pursuant to the laws of the State of

and that the foregoing is a true record of a resolution duly adopted at a meeting of the Board of Directors, and that said meeting was held in accordance with state law and the Bylaws of the above-named Corporation on   , 19   , and that said resolution is now in full force and effect without modification or rescission.

IN WITNESS WHEREOF, I have executed my name as Secretary and have hereunto affixed the corporate seal of the above-named Corporation this   day of   ,

19   .

A True Record.

Attest.

_____
Secretary

RESOLUTION:
ADOPT SEAL

WHEREAS, this Corporation wishes to adopt a corporate seal as its official mark, be it

RESOLVED, that the following mark constitutes the official seal of the Corporation:

The undersigned hereby certifies that he/she is the duly elected and qualified Secretary

and the custodian of the books and records and seal of   ,

a corporation duly formed pursuant to the laws of the State of   ,

and that the foregoing is a true record of a resolution duly adopted at a meeting of the

Board of Directors, and that said meeting was held in accordance with state law and the

Bylaws of the above-named Corporation on   , 19   , and that said

resolution is now in full force and effect without modification or rescission.

IN WITNESS WHEREOF, I have executed my name as Secretary and have hereunto

affixed the corporate seal of the above-named Corporation this   day of   ,

19   .

A True Record.

Attest.

_____
Secretary

RESOLUTION:
AMEND ARTICLES OF INCORPORATION

WHEREAS, this Corporation wishes to change its Articles of Incorporation, be it

RESOLVED, to amend the Articles of Incorporation in accordance with the proposed amendment as set forth on annexed document, and to duly file necessary notices of amendment with the Division of Corporations.

The undersigned hereby certifies that he/she is the duly elected and qualified Secretary and the custodian of the books and records and seal of   ,
a corporation duly formed pursuant to the laws of the State of   ,
and that the foregoing is a true record of a resolution duly adopted at a meeting of the Stockholders, and that said meeting was held in accordance with state law and the Bylaws of the above-named Corporation on   , 19   , and that said resolution is now in full force and effect without modification or rescission.

IN WITNESS WHEREOF, I have executed my name as Secretary and have hereunto affixed the corporate seal of the above-named Corporation this   day of   ,
19   .

A True Record.

Attest.

_____

Secretary

RESOLUTION:
AMEND BYLAWS

WHEREAS, this Corporation wishes to change its Bylaws, be it

RESOLVED, that the Corporation change its Bylaws in accordance with the proposed amendments to Bylaws as annexed hereto, and

FURTHER RESOLVED, that the proper officers of the Corporation file said amended Bylaws with such parties who are, pursuant to law, required to receive or approve same.

The undersigned hereby certifies that he/she is the duly elected and qualified Secretary and the custodian of the books and records and seal of   ,
a corporation duly formed pursuant to the laws of the State of   ,
and that the foregoing is a true record of a resolution duly adopted at a meeting of the Stockholders, and that said meeting was held in accordance with state law and the Bylaws of the above-named Corporation on   , 19   , and that said resolution is now in full force and effect without modification or rescission.

IN WITNESS WHEREOF, I have executed my name as Secretary and have hereunto affixed the corporate seal of the above-named Corporation this   day of   ,
19   .

A True Record.

Attest.

_____
Secretary

RESOLUTION:
AMEND BYLAWS AND FOR SHAREHOLDER APPROVAL

RESOLVED, that, in the judgment of the Board of Directors, it is deemed advisable to

amend the Bylaws to provide   , and for that

purpose to change Sections   of Article   of the said Bylaws to

read as follows:

RESOLVED FURTHER, that a special meeting of the stockholders of this Corporation is

hereby called at the office of the Corporation at

                         on   , 19   , at   .m., to take action upon the

foregoing resolution, and that the Secretary of the Corporation is hereby directed to give

written notice of the said meeting to all stockholders of the Corporation.

The undersigned hereby certifies that he/she is the duly elected and qualified Secretary

and the custodian of the books and records and seal of   ,

a corporation duly formed pursuant to the laws of the State of   ,

and that the foregoing is a true record of a resolution duly adopted at a meeting of the

Board of Directors, and that said meeting was held in accordance with state law and the

Bylaws of the above-named Corporation on   , 19   , and that

said resolution is now in full force and effect without modification or rescission.

IN WITNESS WHEREOF, I have executed my name as Secretary and have hereunto

affixed the corporate seal of the above-named Corporation this   day of   ,

19   .

A True Record.

Attest.

_____
Secretary

RESOLUTION:
AUTHORIZE APPOINTMENT OF DIRECTOR OR OFFICER

Upon motion duly made and seconded, the Board of Directors of

Corporation unanimously adopted the following resolution:

RESOLVED, that   be

appointed the   of

Corporation, and shall hold office until the next annual shareholders' meeting.

shall have the authority to perform the following duties while holding

office:

and such other duties in the management of the corporation as may be required by the

Articles of Incorporation, the Bylaws or by resolution of the Board of Directors of the

corporation.

The undersigned hereby certifies that he/she is the duly elected and qualified Secretary

and the custodian of the books and records and seal of   ,

a corporation duly formed pursuant to the laws of the State of   ,

and that the foregoing is a true record of a resolution duly adopted at a meeting of the

Board of Directors, and that said meeting was held in accordance with state law and the

Bylaws of the above-named Corporation on   , 19   , and that said

resolution is now in full force and effect without modification or rescission.

IN WITNESS WHEREOF, I have executed my name as Secretary and have hereunto

affixed the corporate seal of the above-named Corporation this   day of   ,

19   .

A True Record.

Attest.

_____
Secretary

RESOLUTION:
BLANKET AUTHORITY TO AMEND BYLAWS

WHEREAS, the Stockholders of the Corporation understand the Board of Directors may from time to time deem it necessary to change the Bylaws of the Corporation, be it

RESOLVED, that the Board of Directors is hereby authorized and empowered to amend, alter, change, add to, repeal or rescind any and all Bylaws of said corpration from time to time as the Board of Directors deems proper without action or consent on the part of the stockholders, and be it

FURTHER RESOLVED, that the stockholders reserve the right to revoke the above grant of power to the Directors by resolution duly passed at any subsequent stockholder meeting, but until such revocation, the stockholders shall not exercise their power to amend, alter, change, add to, repeal or rescind the Bylaws of the Corporation presently contained in Article   of said Bylaws.

The undersigned hereby certifies that he/she is the duly elected and qualified Secretary and the custodian of the books and records and seal of   ,
a corporation duly formed pursuant to the laws of the State of   ,
and that the foregoing is a true record of a resolution duly adopted at a meeting of the Stockholders, and that said meeting was held in accordance with state law and the Bylaws of the above-named Corporation on   , 19   , and that said resolution is now in full force and effect without modification or rescission.

IN WITNESS WHEREOF, I have executed my name as Secretary and have hereunto affixed the corporate seal of the above-named Corporation this   day of   ,
19   .

A True Record.

Attest.

_____
Secretary

RESOLUTION:
CHANGE AMOUNT OF AUTHORIZED SHARES

WHEREAS, this Corporation wishes to change the number of authorized shares, be it

RESOLVED, to change the number of authorized shares of common stock of the Corporation from   shares to   shares, and to obtain such authorizations as are necessary from the Division of Corporations and to pay any fees associated therewith.

The undersigned hereby certifies that he/she is the duly elected and qualified Secretary and the custodian of the books and records and seal of   ,
a corporation duly formed pursuant to the laws of the State of   ,
and that the foregoing is a true record of a resolution duly adopted at a meeting of the Stockholders, and that said meeting was held in accordance with state law and the Bylaws of the above-named Corporation on   , 19   , and that said resolution is now in full force and effect without modification or rescission.

IN WITNESS WHEREOF, I have executed my name as Secretary and have hereunto affixed the corporate seal of the above-named Corporation this   day of   ,
19   .

A True Record.

Attest.

_____
Secretary

RESOLUTION:

CHANGE CORPORATE ADDRESS

RESOLVED, that the Corporation change its official address from

to   , and that said change

of address be duly filed with the Department of Corporations and such further parties who

shall be entitled to notice or wherein notice is desirable as in the best interests of the

Corporation.

The undersigned hereby certifies that he/she is the duly elected and qualified Secretary

and the custodian of the books and records and seal of   ,

a corporation duly formed pursuant to the laws of the State of   ,

and that the foregoing is a true record of a resolution duly adopted at a meeting of the

Board of Directors, and that said meeting was held in accordance with state law and the

Bylaws of the above-named Corporation on   , 19   , and that said

resolution is now in full force and effect without modification or rescission.

IN WITNESS WHEREOF, I have executed my name as Secretary and have hereunto

affixed the corporate seal of the above-named Corporation this   day of   ,

19   .

A True Record.

Attest.

_____

Secretary

RESOLUTION:
CHANGE CORPORATE NAME

RESOLUTION:

That the Corporation change its corporate name from

to   ; and that said change of name be

duly filed with the Department of Corporations in accordance with State law and such

other governmental agencies as may be required to be notified of or to approve said name

change.

The undersigned hereby certifies that he/she is the duly elected and qualified Secretary

and the custodian of the books and records and seal of   ,

a corporation duly formed pursuant to the laws of the State of   ,

and that the foregoing is a true record of a resolution duly adopted at a meeting of the

Board of Directors, and that said meeting was held in accordance with state law and the

Bylaws of the above-named Corporation on   , 19   , and that said

resolution is now in full force and effect without modification or rescission.

IN WITNESS WHEREOF, I have executed my name as Secretary and have hereunto

affixed the corporate seal of the above-named Corporation this   day of   ,

19   .

A True Record.

Attest.

_____

Secretary

RESOLUTION:
CHANGE FISCAL YEAR

WHEREAS, the Corporation would gain certain accounting and tax benefits from a change in fiscal year; be it

RESOLVED, that the Corporation change its fiscal year from the twelve month period ending   of each year to the twelve month period ending   of each year, and that said change of fiscal year be recorded with the Department of Corporations.

The undersigned hereby certifies that he/she is the duly elected and qualified Secretary and the custodian of the books and records and seal of   ,
a corporation duly formed pursuant to the laws of the State of   ,
and that the foregoing is a true record of a resolution duly adopted at a meeting of the Board of Directors, and that said meeting was held in accordance with state law and the Bylaws of the above-named Corporation on   , 19   , and that said resolution is now in full force and effect without modification or rescission.

IN WITNESS WHEREOF, I have executed my name as Secretary and have hereunto affixed the corporate seal of the above-named Corporation this   day of   ,
19   .

A True Record.

Attest.

_____
Secretary

RESOLUTION:
CHANGE NUMBER OF AUTHORIZED SHARES

RESOLVED, to change the number of authorized shares of common stock of the

Corporation from   shares to   shares, and to obtain such

authorizations as are necessary from the Division of Corporations and to pay any fees

associated therewith.

The undersigned hereby certifies that he/she is the duly elected and qualified Secretary

and the custodian of the books and records and seal of   ,

a corporation duly formed pursuant to the laws of the State of   ,

and that the foregoing is a true record of a resolution duly adopted at a meeting of the

Board of Directors, and that said meeting was held in accordance with state law and the

Bylaws of the above-named Corporation on   , 19   , and that said

resolution is now in full force and effect without modification or rescission.

IN WITNESS WHEREOF, I have executed my name as Secretary and have hereunto

affixed the corporate seal of the above-named Corporation this   day of   ,

19   .

A True Record.

Attest.

_____
Secretary

RESOLUTION:
DISSOLVE CORPORATION AND FOR SHAREHOLDER APPROVAL

RESOLVED, that in the judgment of the Board of Directors it is deemed advisable that this Corporation should be dissolved; and as required by law, it is ordered that a meeting of those stockholders of said Corporation having voting power to take action upon this resolution is hereby called, to be held at the office of said Corporation at

      /   , on   , 19   , at   .m., and

RESOLVED FURTHER, that the Secretary of this Corporation is hereby authorized and directed, within   (   ) days after its adoption, this resolution be mailed to each stockholder of this Corporation, and also within   (   ) days after the adoption of this resolution, to cause notice of the time appointed for said meeting to be inserted in a newspaper published in the County of   /

State of   , once a week, for at least   (   ) successive weeks preceding the meeting.

The undersigned hereby certifies that he/she is the duly elected and qualified Secretary and the custodian of the books and records and seal of   /

a corporation duly formed pursuant to the laws of the State of   /

and that the foregoing is a true record of a resolution duly adopted at a meeting of the Board of Directors, and that said meeting was held in accordance with state law and the Bylaws of the above-named Corporation on   , 19   , and that said resolution is now in full force and effect without modification or rescission.

IN WITNESS WHEREOF, I have executed my name as Secretary and have hereunto affixed the corporate seal of the above-named Corporation this   day of   /

19   .

A True Record.

Attest.

_____
Secretary

RESOLUTION:
EXTEND APPOINTMENT

WHEREAS,   has had an appointment to serve the

Corporation as   for a   year period due to terminate on

     , 19   , and

WHEREAS,   has requested an extension of said

appointment and an extension would also be to the advantage of the Corporation; be it

RESOLVED, that the Corporation extend the appointment of

for a period of   , upon such compensation, benefits and terms as

presently in effect.

The undersigned hereby certifies that he/she is the duly elected and qualified Secretary

and the custodian of the books and records and seal of   ,

a corporation duly formed pursuant to the laws of the State of   ,

and that the foregoing is a true record of a resolution duly adopted at a meeting of the

Board of Directors, and that said meeting was held in accordance with state law and the

Bylaws of the above-named Corporation on   , 19   , and that said

resolution is now in full force and effect without modification or rescission.

IN WITNESS WHEREOF, I have executed my name as Secretary and have hereunto

affixed the corporate seal of the above-named Corporation this   day of   ,

19   .

A True Record.

Attest.

_____

RESOLUTION:
FILL VACANCY ON BOARD

RESOLVED, that   is hereby appointed a director of the Corporation until the next annual stockholders' meeting, to fill the vacancy caused by the resignation of   .

The undersigned hereby certifies that he/she is the duly elected and qualified Secretary and the custodian of the books and records and seal of   , a corporation duly formed pursuant to the laws of the State of   , and that the foregoing is a true record of a resolution duly adopted at a meeting of the Board of Directors, and that said meeting was held in accordance with state law and the Bylaws of the above-named Corporation on   , 19   , and that said resolution is now in full force and effect without modification or rescission.

IN WITNESS WHEREOF, I have executed my name as Secretary and have hereunto affixed the corporate seal of the above-named Corporation this   day of   , 19   .

A True Record.

Attest.

_____
Secretary

RESOLUTION:
OBTAIN "S" CORPORATION STATUS

WHEREAS, there would be certain tax and financial benefits to the shareholders of the Corporation upon an election to have the Corporation qualify as an "S" Corporation pursuant to Section 1362 of the Internal Revenue Code; be it

RESOLVED, to qualify the Corporation as an "S" Corporation pursuant to Section 1362 of the Internal Revenue Code.

The undersigned hereby certifies that he/she is the duly elected and qualified Secretary and the custodian of the books and records and seal of   ,
a corporation duly formed pursuant to the laws of the State of   ,
and that the foregoing is a true record of a resolution duly adopted at a meeting of the Stockholders, and that said meeting was held in accordance with state law and the Bylaws of the above-named Corporation on   , 19   , and that said resolution is now in full force and effect without modification or rescission.

IN WITNESS WHEREOF, I have executed my name as Secretary and have hereunto affixed the corporate seal of the above-named Corporation this   day of   ,
19   .

A True Record.

Attest.

_____
Secretary

RESOLUTION:
REMOVE AN OFFICER OR DIRECTOR

RESOLVED, that   is hereby removed from office as

of this Corporation, effective herewith, and

RESOLVED FURTHER, that the Secretary of this Corporation is hereby directed to give

notice of such removal to the said   .

The undersigned hereby certifies that he/she is the duly elected and qualified Secretary

and the custodian of the books and records and seal of   ,

a corporation duly formed pursuant to the laws of the State of   ,

and that the foregoing is a true record of a resolution duly adopted at a meeting of the

Board of Directors, and that said meeting was held in accordance with state law and the

Bylaws of the above-named Corporation on   , 19   , and that said

resolution is now in full force and effect without modification or rescission.

IN WITNESS WHEREOF, I have executed my name as Secretary and have hereunto

affixed the corporate seal of the above-named Corporation this   day of   ,

19   .

A True Record.

Attest.

_____
Secretary

RESOLUTION:
REQUEST RESIGNATION OF OFFICER

RESOLVED, that   is hereby requested to resign as

of the Corporation, effective immediately, and the

Secretary of the Corporation is hereby directed to send a copy of this resolution to the said

.

The undersigned hereby certifies that he/she is the duly elected and qualified Secretary

and the custodian of the books and records and seal of   ,

a corporation duly formed pursuant to the laws of the State of   ,

and that the foregoing is a true record of a resolution duly adopted at a meeting of the

Board of Directors, and that said meeting was held in accordance with state law and the

Bylaws of the above-named Corporation on   , 19   , and that said

resolution is now in full force and effect without modification or rescission.

IN WITNESS WHEREOF, I have executed my name as Secretary and have hereunto

affixed the corporate seal of the above-named Corporation this   day of   ,

19   .

A True Record.

Attest.

_____

Secretary

RESOLUTION:
TERMINATE FOREIGN CORPORATION STATUS

WHEREAS, the Corporation has or shall discontinue the conduct of business within the

State of   ; be it

RESOLVED, to have the Corporation terminate its status as a foreign Corporation in the

State of   .

The undersigned hereby certifies that he/she is the duly elected and qualified Secretary

and the custodian of the books and records and seal of   ,

a corporation duly formed pursuant to the laws of the State of   ,

and that the foregoing is a true record of a resolution duly adopted at a meeting of the

Board of Directors, and that said meeting was held in accordance with state law and the

Bylaws of the above-named Corporation on   , 19   , and that said

resolution is now in full force and effect without modification or rescission.

IN WITNESS WHEREOF, I have executed my name as Secretary and have hereunto

affixed the corporate seal of the above-named Corporation this   day of   ,

19   .

A True Record.

Attest.

_____
Secretary

RESOLUTION:
TERMINATE "S" CORPORATION STATUS

WHEREAS, there are no longer benefits to the shareholders of the Corporation to have the Corporation qualify as an "S" Corporation, and it is desirable to have the Corporation operate as a "C" Corporation; be it

RESOLVED, to terminate the Corporation as an "S" Corporation under Section 1362 of the Internal Revenue Code.

The undersigned hereby certifies that he/she is the duly elected and qualified Secretary and the custodian of the books and records and seal of   ,
a corporation duly formed pursuant to the laws of the State of   ,
and that the foregoing is a true record of a resolution duly adopted at a meeting of the Stockholders, and that said meeting was held in accordance with state law and the Bylaws of the above-named Corporation on   , 19   , and that said resolution is now in full force and effect without modification or rescission.

IN WITNESS WHEREOF, I have executed my name as Secretary and have hereunto affixed the corporate seal of the above-named Corporation this   day of   ,
19   .

A True Record.

Attest.

_____
Secretary

Section Three
Minutes of Meetings

Form M301   Contains the minutes of the first meeting of the Board of Directors.

Form M302   Contains the minutes of the annual meeting of stockholders.

Form M303   Contains the minutes of a combined meeting of stockholders and directors.

Form M304   Contains the minutes of a Board of Directors' meeting.

Form M305   Contains the minutes of the corporation's organizational meeting of the Board of Directors.

Form M306   Contains the minutes of a special meeting of the corporation's directors.

Form M307   Contains the minutes of a special meeting of the corporation stockholders.

Form N301   Notifies the shareholders of the time and place of the annual meeting.

Form N302   Notifies the directors of the corporation of a meeting.

Form N303   Notifies the incorporators and directors of the organizational meeting.

Form N304   Waiver by shareholders of being notified of annual meeting.

Form N305   Notifies director of a special meeting.

Form N306   Notifies shareholders of a special meeting.

Form R301   Calls a shareholders' meeting to elect a new board of directors and transact any other necessary business.

Form R302	Changes the date of the corporation's annual meeting.

Form R303	Establishes the date for shareholders to be eligible to vote at the annual meeting.

Form R304	Calls for a special meeting of shareholders to elect directors of the corporation.

Form R305	Calls for a special meeting of shareholders to consider a specific resolution.

Form W301	Waives notice of combined meeting of shareholders and directors by single shareholder or director.

Form W302	Waives notice of annual meeting by individual shareholder.

Form W303	Waives notice of directors' meeting by entire Board of Directors.

Form W304	Waives notice of organization meeting by incorporators and directors.

Form W305	Gives written unanimous consent by all outstanding shareholders to a specific resolution adopted by the Board of Directors in place of a meeting.

MINUTES, FIRST MEETING OF DIRECTORS

_____

The first meeting of the Board of Directors of

Corporation was held at   , in the City of   ,

State of   , on the   day of   , 19   ,   at

      .m.

There were present: ,   ,

and   , being all of the directors of

Corporation.

Upon motion duly made, seconded and carried,   acted as

temporary chairman, and   acted as temporary secretary of the

meeting.

The Secretary put forth and read a waiver of notice of the meeting, signed by all the

directors.

The minutes of the meeting of incorporators and subscribers to the capital stock were

read and approved.

Upon motion duly made, seconded and carried, it was

RESOLVED, that the acts of the incorporators of

Corporation,   and   , jointly and severally, for and on behalf of the Corporation, are hereby approved, ratified and adopted as acts of the Corporation, in the same manner as if each and every such act has been done pursuant to the specific authorization of the Corporation.

Upon motion duly made, seconded and carried, it was

RESOLVED, that all action taken by the incorporators, stockholders and subscribers to capital stock of the Corporation at the organization meeting held at

on the   day of   , 19   , be and

the same are hereby approved and ratified to the full extent that approval and ratification by this Board of Directors is necessary or proper.

Upon motion duly made, seconded and carried, it was

RESOLVED, that the Treasurer is hereby authorized to pay or reimburse all fees and expenses incident to and necessary for the organization of the Corporation, and to procure and pay for the proper corporate books.

Upon motion duly made, seconded and carried, it was

RESOLVED, that the Bylaws for the regulation and management of the affairs of the Corporation, which were read and approved and adopted article by article be filed with the minutes of this meeting and authenticated as the corporate Bylaws by the signature of the Secretary of this meeting.

Upon motion duly made, seconded and carried, it was

RESOLVED, that an election be held to choose a Chairman of the Board of Directors, a

President, an Executive Vice President, a Vice President, a Secretary-Treasurer, to serve for a period of one year and thereafter until their respective successors shall be elected and qualify.

The following persons were nominated officers of the Corporation:

Name	Office
_____	_____
_____	_____
_____	_____
_____	_____
_____	_____

The Chairman announced that the aforementioned persons had been elected to the office set opposite their respective names.

Each of the officers so elected thereupon accepted the office to which elected as aforestated.

_____ moved to consider the salaries of the officers of the Corporation of the year commencing _____ , 19___ . The motion was duly seconded and carried. The Chairman announced that the officer whose salary was being considered would not participate in the vote, and that the salary of each officer would be considered separately.

_____ , President, having left the meeting, it was on motion duly made, seconded and carried:

That the salary of   as President of

Corporation, beginning   , 19   , and ending   , 19   ,

be fixed at   Dollars ($) per year, payable in

installments of   Dollars ($) on the   day of

each and every   .

The salary of   as President of

Corporation, having been duly voted upon,   was recalled to the

meeting.

, Vice President of the Corporation then left the meeting.

, Vice President, having left the meeting, it was on motion duly

made, seconded and carried:

That the salary of   as Vice President of

Corporation, beginning   , 19   , and ending   , 19   ,

be fixed at   Dollars ($) per year, payable in

installments of   Dollars ($) on the   day of

each and every   .

The salary of   as Vice President of

Corporation, having been duly voted upon,   was recalled to the

meeting.

, Secretary-Treasurer of the Corporation, then left the meeting.

, Secretary-Treasurer, having left the meeting, it was on motion duly made, seconded and carried:

That the salary of   , Secretary-Treasurer of

Corporation, beginning   , 19   , and ending   , 19   ,

be fixed at   Dollars ($) per year, payable in

installments of   Dollars ($) on the

day of each and every   .

The salary of   , Secretary-Treasurer of

Corporation, having been duly voted upon,   was recalled to

the meeting.

On motions duly made and seconded it was resolved

1.   That the seal, an impression whereof is hereto attached, be adopted as the corporate seal of this Corporation.

2.   A form of stock certificate was presented and adopted.

3.   That the stock book and transfer book presented to the Board at this meeting are hereby adopted as the stock book and transfer book of the Corporation.

4.   That the Corporation shall act as its own transfer agent, and

5.   That the President shall have the power when necessary to employ one or more transfer clerks, or to assign the duties of a transfer clerk to one or more officers or employees of the Corporation, furthermore to discharge the transfer clerk or clerks, or to revoke the duties of transfer clerk granted to any officer or employee.

6.   That the Board of Directors is hereby authorized and directed to issue and sell, at a consideration fixed by the Board, however, at no less than the par

value of the stock, the entire unsubscribed and unissued authorized capital stock of this Corporation, amounting to   shares of Common Stock with a par value of Dollar(s) per share; and

7.   That the President and Secretary are directed to take all necessary action to comply with the Securities Laws of the United States and the State of before issuing or selling any of said stock.

8.   That the Board of Directors is hereby authorized and directed to issue the remainder of the unissued authorized capital stock of this Corporation, from time to time as may be desirable in its discretion, upon payment therefor of a good and fair consideration fixed by the Board.

WHEREAS,   has offered to purchase all the unsubscribed and unissued shares of common stock of Corporation for the price of $ per share, payable in cash,

AND WHEREAS, the Board of Directors of this Corporation deem such a sale desirable:

That the Board of Directors is hereby authorized to accept the offer of and to issue to said offerer   shares of common stock, and the certificate evidencing the same upon full payment of the agreed price.

9.   That the principal office of the Corporation in   be established and maintained at   , in the City of

10.   That the fiscal year of the Corporation begin on the first day of

in each year.

11. That the   Bank located at

(hereinafter "Bank") is hereby designated as a depository of this Corporation and that the officers and agents of this Corporation are hereby authorized to deposit any and all of the funds of this Corporation in said Bank either at its head office or at any of its branches.

12. That any funds of this Corporation deposited in said Bank be subject to withdrawal or charge at any time and from time to time upon checks, notes, drafts, bills of exchange, acceptances, undertakings, or other instruments or orders for the payment of money when made, signed, drawn, accepted or endorsed on behalf of this Corporation by any two of the following officers: President, Vice President, Secretary-Treasurer.

13. That the Bank is hereby authorized to pay any such instrument or make any such charge and also to receive the same from the payee or any other holder without inquiry as to the circumstances of issue or the disposition of the proceeds even if drawn to the individual order of any signing person, or payable to said Bank or others for his account, or tendered in payment of his individual obligation, and whether drawn against an account in the name of this Corporation or in the name of any officer or agent of this Corporation as such.

14. That any two of the following: the President, Vice President, Secretary-Treasurer are hereby authorized on behalf of this Corporation:

A. To borrow money and to obtain credit for the Corporation from the Bank on any terms and to make and deliver notes, drafts, acceptances, instruments of guaranty, agreements and any other obligations of this

Corporation therefor in form satisfactory to the Bank.

B. To pledge or assign and deliver, as security for money borrowed or credit obtained, stocks, bonds, bills receivable, accounts, mortgages, merchandise, bills-of-lading, warehouse receipts, insurance policies, certificates, and any other property held by or belonging to the Corporation with full authority to endorse, assign, or guarantee the same in the name of the Corporation.

C. To discount any bills receivable or any paper held by the Corporation with full authority to endorse the same in the name of the Corporation.

D. To withdraw from the Bank and give receipt for, or to authorize the Bank to deliver to bearer or to one or more designated persons, all or any documents and securities or other property held by it, whether held as collateral security or for safekeeping or for any other purpose.

E. To authorize the Bank to purchase or sell for account of the Corporation stocks, bonds and other securities, and

F. To execute and deliver all instruments required by the Bank in connection with any of the foregoing matters and affix thereto the seal of this Corporation.

15. That the Secretary or any other officer of this Corporation is hereby authorized to certify to the Bank the names of the present officers of this Corporation and other persons authorized to sign for it and the offices respectively held by them, together with specimens of their signatures, and in case of any change of any holder of any such office or holders of any such offices, the fact of such change and the names of any new officers and the

offices respectively held by them, together with specimens of their signatures; and the Bank is hereby authorized to honor any instrument signed by any new officer or officers in respect of whom it has received any such certificate or certificates with the same force and effect as if said officer or said officers were named in the foregoing resolutions in the place of any person or persons with the same title or titles.

16. That the Bank be promptly notified in writing by the Secretary or any officer of this Corporation of any change in these resolutions, such notice to be given to each office of the Bank in which any account of this Corporation may be kept, and that until it has actually received such notice in writing it is authorized to act in pursuance of these resolutions, and that until it has actually so received such notice it shall be indemnified and saved harmless from any loss suffered or liability incurred by it in continuing to act in pursuance of these resolutions, not withstanding, that these resolutions may have been changed.

17. That, beginning with the present meeting, the fees of non-salaried members of the Board of Directors be fixed at $ per meeting.

Upon motion duly made, seconded and carried, it was further resolved

18. That   be engaged to make the annual audit of the books of this Corporation for the year ending   , 19   , and that

be paid the sum of

Dollars ($) for such services; and that the proper officers of this Corporation are hereby authorized and directed to execute a written retainer for said services of   .

There being no further business, a motion was duly made, seconded and carried that the meeting be adjourned.

_____   _____
President   Secretary

MINUTES OF ANNUAL MEETING OF STOCKHOLDERS

_____

The annual meeting of stockholders of   was held

at   at

.m., on   , 19   .

The meeting was called to order by   , President, who

chaired the meeting, and   , Secretary, kept the record of the meeting.

The Secretary stated that the following stockholders were present in person:

Names   Number of Shares

_____   _____

_____   _____

_____   _____

_____   _____

and that the following stockholders were represented by proxy:

Names   Number of Proxies   Number of Shares

_____   _____   _____

_____   _____   _____

_____   _____   _____

_____   _____   _____

_____   _____   _____

The Chairman then reported that there were present in person and represented by proxy the number of shares necessary to constitute a quorum to conduct business.

The proxies presented were directed to be filed with the Secretary of the meeting.

The Chairman then stated that the next business to come before the meeting was the election of the Board of Directors to serve for the upcoming year.

The following were nominated as directors:

_____

_____

_____

No other persons were nominated.

Upon motion duly made, seconded and unanimously carried, the nominations were closed.

The ballots of the stockholders were presented and the Secretary reported that

_____,   and   had

received a plurality of the votes.

The Chairman then declared that the aforementioned persons were duly elected directors of the Corporation to hold office for the upcoming year.

MINUTES OF COMBINED MEETING
OF
STOCKHOLDERS AND DIRECTORS

A combined meeting of Stockholders and Directors was held at the office of the

Corporation at   on

19   , at   .m.

The following Directors were present at the meeting:

_____   _____

_____   _____

_____   _____

being a quorum of the Directors of the Corporation.

The following Shareholders were present in person or by proxy at the meeting:

_____   _____

_____   _____

_____   _____

being a quorum of the Shareholders of the Corporation.

                    , President of the Corporation, acted as Chairman of the

meeting, and   , Secretary of the Corporation, acted as

Secretary of the meeting.

The Secretary presented notice or waiver of notice of the meeting, signed by all interested parties.

The meeting, having been duly convened, was ready to proceed with its business, whereupon it was resolved:

The Secretary announced that _____ shares of common stock had been voted in favor of the foregoing resolution(s) and _____ shares of common stock had been voted against the resolution(s), said vote representing more than _____ % of the outstanding shares entitled to vote thereon.

The President thereupon declared that the resolution(s) had been duly adopted.

There being no further business, upon motion, the meeting was adjourned.

_____
Secretary

MINUTES OF DIRECTORS' MEETINGS

A regular meeting of the Board of Directors of

was held at   on   ,

19   , at   .m.

The following were present and participating at the meeting:

---

being all the directors of the Corporation.

, President of the Corporation, acted as Chairman of the

meeting, and   , Secretary of the Corporation, acted as Secretary of the

meeting.

The Secretary put forth a waiver of notice of the meeting, signed by all the directors, and accordingly filed the waiver of notice with the minutes of the meeting.

The Chairman stated that a quorum of the directors was present, and that the meeting, having been duly convened, could transact business.

The minutes of the regular meeting of the directors held on   ,

19   , were read and approved.

WHEREAS, the accumulated surplus of the Corporation is

Dollars ($).

RESOLVED, that a dividend of   cents per share is hereby declared on

the outstanding capital stock of this Corporation, that said dividend will be paid on

, 19   , to stockholders of record at the close of business on

, 19   ; and

RESOLVED FURTHER, that the Secretary is hereby authorized and instructed to notify

said stockholders of the declaration of said dividend, and the Treasurer is hereby

authorized and instructed to pay said dividend on said date.

A motion was duly made and carried to consider the salaries of the officers of the

Corporation for the year commencing on   , 19   . The Chairman stated

that the officer whose salary was being considerated would not participate in the vote, and

that the salary of each officer would be considered separately.

, President, having left the meeting, it was on motion

duly made, seconded and carried:

That the salary of   , as President of the Corporation, be fixed

at   Dollars ($) per

year.

The salary of   , as President of the Corporation, having been

duly voted upon,   was recalled to the meeting.

, Vice President of the Corporation, then left the meeting.

, Vice President having left the meeting, it was on motion duly made, seconded and carried:

That the salary of   , as Vice President of the Corporation, be fixed at   Dollars ($) per year.

The salary of   , as Vice President of the Corporation, having been duly voted upon,   was recalled to the meeting.

, Treasurer of the Corporation, then left the meeting.

, Treasurer having left the meeting, it was on motion duly made, seconded and carried:

That the salary of   , as Treasurer of the Corporation, be fixed at   Dollars ($) per year.

The salary of   , as Treasurer of the Corporation, having been duly voted upon,   was recalled to the meeting.

, Secretary of the Corporation, then left the meeting.

, Secretary having left the meeting, it was on motion duly made, seconded and carried:

That the salary of   , as Secretary of the Corporation, be fixed at

Dollars ($)
per year.

   The salary of   , as Secretary of the Corporation, having been
duly voted upon,   was recalled to the meeting.

   There being no further business, the meeting was adjourned.

_____
Chairman

_____
Secretary

MINUTES OF ORGANIZATION MEETING
OF BOARD OF DIRECTORS OF

———————————————

The organizational meeting of the Board of Directors of

was held at   on   ,

19   , at   .m.

Present was   ,   ,   ,

being the persons designated as the Directors in the Articles of Incorporation.

acted as temporary Chairman of the meeting and

acted as temporary Secretary.

The Chairman stated that the meeting had been duly called by the Incorporators of the

Corporation.

The Chairman announced that the Articles of Incorporation of the Corporation had

been duly filed with the State of   on   ,

19   . The Certificate of Incorporation and a copy of said Articles of Incorporation were

directed to be inserted in the Minutes and made a part thereof.

A proposed form of Bylaws for the regulation and the management of the affairs of the

Corporation was put forth at the meeting. The Bylaws were read and deliberated and,

upon motion duly made and seconded, it was:

RESOLVED, that the form of Bylaws of the Corporation, as put forth in this meeting, a copy of which is ordered to be inserted in the Minute Book of the Corporation, and the same are hereby approved and adopted as the Bylaws of the Corporation.

The following persons were nominated officers of the Corporation to serve until their respective successors are chosen and qualify:

PRESIDENT:

VICE PRESIDENT:

SECRETARY:

TREASURER:

The Chairman announced that said persons had been elected to the office set opposite their respective names.

The President thereupon took the chair and the Secretary immediately assumed the discharge of the duties of that office.

The President then announced that there were a number of organizational matters to be deliberated at the meeting and a number of resolutions to be approved and adopted by the Board of Directors.

The form of stock certificates was then exhibited at the meeting. Thereupon, a motion duly made and seconded, it was:

RESOLVED, that the form of stock certificates put forth at this meeting be, and the same is hereby adopted and approved as the stock certificate of the Corporation, a specimen copy of the stock certificate to be attached with these Minutes.

FURTHER RESOLVED, that the officers are hereby authorized and directed to pay or reimburse the payment of all fees and expenses incident to and necessary for the organization of this Corporation.

The Board of Directors then considered the opening of a corporate bank account to serve as a depository for the funds of the Corporation. Following deliberation, on motion duly made and seconded, it was:

RESOLVED, that the Treasurer be authorized and directed to open an account with and to deposit all funds of the Corporation, all drafts, checks and notes of the Corporation payable on said account to be made in the corporate name signed by   .

FURTHER RESOLVED, that officers are hereby authorized to execute such resolutions (including formal Bank Resolutions), documents and other instruments as may be necessary or advisable in opening or continuing said bank account. A copy of the applicable printed form of Bank Resolution hereby adopted to supplement these Minutes is ordered attached to the Minutes of this meeting.

It is reported that the following persons have made an offer to transfer the property listed below in exchange for the following shares of the stock of the Corporation:

Name	Payment Consideration, or Property	Number of Shares

Upon motion duly made and seconded, it was:

RESOLVED, that acceptance of the offer of the aforementioned persons is in the best interest of the Corporation and necessary for carrying out the corporate business, and in the judgment of the Board of Directors, the assets proposed to be transferred to the Corporation are reasonably worth the amount of consideration deemed therefore, and the same hereby is accepted, and that upon receipt of the consideration indicated above, the President and the Secretary are authorized and directed to issue certificates of fully paid, nonassessable capital stock of this Corporation in the amounts indicated to the aforementioned persons.

To insure the payment of expenses of incorporation and organization for the Corporation, on motion duly made, seconded and unanimously carried, the following resolution was adopted:

RESOLVED, that the President and the Secretary and/or Treasurer of Corporation be and they are hereby authorized and directed to pay the expenses of this Corporation, including attorney's fees for incorporation, and to reimburse the persons who have made disbursement thereof.

After deliberation of the appropriate issues with regard to the tax year and accounting basis, on motion duly made, seconded and unanimously carried, the following resolution was adopted:

RESOLVED, that the first fiscal year of the Corporation shall commence on
                and end on   .

FURTHER RESOLVED, that the President be and is hereby authorized and directed to enter into employment contracts with certain employees, such contract shall be for the term and the rate stated in the attached Employment Agreements.

FURTHER RESOLVED, that it shall be the policy of the Corporation to reimburse each employee or to pay directly on his behalf all expenses incidental to his attendance at conventions and seminars as may be approved by the President. Reimbursement shall include full reimbursement for commercial and private transportation, expenses, plus other necessary and ordinary out-of-pocket expenses incidental to the said travel, including meals and lodging.

A deliberation was then held concerning the immediate commencement of business operations as a Corporation and it was then decided that business operations of the Corporation would commence as of

It was agreed that no fixed date would be set for holding meetings of the Board of Directors except the regular meetings to be held immediately after the annual meetings of shareholders as provided in the Bylaws of the Corporation but that meetings of the Directors would be periodically called by the President and Secretary or others pursuant to the Bylaws.

Upon motion duly made, seconded and unanimously carried, it was:

RESOLVED, that the officers of the Corporation are hereby authorized and empowered to do any and all things necessary to conduct the business of the Corporation as set forth in the Articles of Incorporation and Bylaws of the Corporation.

Upon motion duly made, seconded and unanimously carried, the following resolution was adopted:

RESOLVED, that, if required, _____ be, and hereby is, appointed Resident Agent in the State of _____ . The office of the Resident Agent will be located at _____ .

The Chairman then announced at the meeting the question of electing the provisions of Section 1244 of the Internal Revenue Code. He stated that this Section permits ordinary loss treatment when either the holder of Section 1244 stock sells or exchanges such stock at a loss or when such stock becomes worthless. After deliberation, the following preamble was announced and the following resolution was unanimously approved:

RESOLVED, that:

WHEREAS, this Corporation qualifies as a small business corporation as defined in Section 1244, but

WHEREAS, the Board of Directors are concerned over future tax law changes modifying Section 1244 as presently enacted (subsequent to the Revenue Act of 1978) and thus desire to safeguard this Corporation's 1244 election by complying with prior law as well as present law, and

WHEREAS, pursuant to the requirements of Section 1244 and the Regulations issued thereunder, the following plan has been presented to the Corporation by the Board of Directors of the Corporation:

    (a)   The plan as hereafter set forth shall, upon its adoption by the Board of Directors of the Corporation, immediately become effective.

    (b)   No more than _____ shares of common stock are authorized to be issued under this plan, and such stock shall have a par value of $ _____ per share.

(c)   Stock authorized under this plan shall be issued only in exchange for money, or property subject to monetary valuation other than capital stock, securities or services rendered or to be rendered. The aggregate dollar amount to be received for such stock shall not exceed $1,000,000, and the sum of each aggregate dollar amount and the equity capital of the Corporation (determined on the date of adoption of the plan) shall not exceed $1,000,000.

(d)   Any stock options granted during the life of this plan which apply to the stock issuable hereunder shall apply solely to such stock and to no other and must be exercised within the period in which the plan is effective.

(e)   Such other action as may be necessary shall be taken by the Corporation to qualify the stock to be offered and issued under this plan as "Section 1244 Stock," as such term is defined in the Internal Revenue Code and the regulations issued thereunder.

NOW, THEREFORE, said plan to issue Section 1244 Stock is adopted by the Corporation and the appropriate officers of the Corporation are authorized and directed to take all actions deemed by them necessary to carry out the intent and purpose of the recited plan.

There being no further business requiring Board action or consideration, the meeting was adjourned.

Dated:

_____
Secretary

MINUTES OF SPECIAL MEETING OF DIRECTORS

A special meeting of the Board of Directors of   was
held at the office of the Corporation,   ,
on   , 19   , at   .m.

The following directors were present and participating at the meeting:

---

being all of the directors of the Corporation.

, President of the Corporation, acted as Chairman of the
meeting, and   , Secretary of the Corporation, acted as Secretary of the
meeting.

The Secretary put forth and read a waiver of notice of the meeting signed by all the
directors, and accordingly, filed a copy of the waiver with the minutes of the meeting.

The Chairman stated that a quorum of the directors was present, and that the meeting,
having been duly convened, could transact business.

On the motion duly made and seconded, and after due deliberation, the following
resolution was adopted:

There being no further business, the meeting was adjourned.

Secretary

MINUTES OF SPECIAL MEETING OF STOCKHOLDERS

_____

A special meeting of the stockholders was duly called and held at

_____ , in the City of _____ , in the State of _____ ,

on _____ , 19___ , at _____ .m.

The meeting was called to order by _____ , the President of the

Corporation, and _____ , the Secretary of the Corporation, kept the

records of the meeting and its proceedings.

The Secretary noted that stockholders owning _____ shares were present in

person and stockholders owning _____ shares were represented by proxy, the

aggregate amount representing more than _____ percent of the outstanding stock

entitled to vote on the amendment to the articles of incorporation proposed at the meeting.

The secretary stated that the following stockholders were present in person:

Names	Number of Shares
_____	_____
_____	_____
_____	_____

and that the following stockholders were represented by proxy:

Names	Names of Proxies	Number of Shares
_____	_____	_____
_____	_____	_____
_____	_____	_____

The Chairman then reported that there were present in person and represented by proxy the number of shares necessary to constitute a quorum to conduct business.

The Secretary put forth and read a waiver of notice of the meeting signed by each stockholder entitled to notice of the meeting, said waiver of notice together with a copy of the proxies submitted at the meeting were directed to be filed with the minutes of the meeting.

On the motion duly made and seconded, and after due deliberation, the following resolution was made:

A vote was taken which showed:

In Favor of Motion

_____, representing   shares

_____, representing   shares

_____, representing   shares

Opposed to Motion

_____, representing   shares

_____, representing   shares

Not Voting on Motion

_____, representing   shares

   The Secretary announced that   shares of common stock had been voted in
favor of the said resolution and   shares of common stock had been voted
against said resolution, said vote representing more than   percent of
outstanding shares in attendance and entitled to vote thereon.

   The President thereafter declared that the resolution had been duly adopted.

   There being no further business, upon motion duly made, the meeting adjourned.

_____
Secretary

NOTICE OF ANNUAL SHAREHOLDERS' MEETING

Notice is hereby given that the annual meeting of shareholders of

shall be held on   , 19   , at   .m., in

the offices of the Corporation at   ,

in the City of   .

The shareholders will deliberate and take action on the following matters:

    1.   The election of a new Board of Directors for the year beginning   ,

           19   , and ending   , 19   .

    2.   Transact such other business as may properly come before the meeting or any

           adjournment thereof.

Only those shareholders who were shareholders of record at the close of business on

        , 19   , will be entitled to vote in person or by proxy at the meeting or

any adjournment thereof.

           By order of the Board of Directors

           of   Corporation

           _____

           Secretary

Dated:

NOTICE OF MEETING — DIRECTORS

A meeting of the Board of Directors of   , will be held

on   , 19   , at   .m., in the offices of the

Corporation located at   for the

following matter:

Dated:

_____

Secretary

NOTICE OF ORGANIZATION MEETING
OF INCORPORATORS AND DIRECTORS

TO: _____

_____

_____

You are hereby notified that:

We, the undersigned, do hereby constitute a majority of the directors named in the

Articles of Incorporation of _____, a corporation.

Pursuant to state law, we are hereby calling an organization meeting of the Board of

Directors and incorporators named in the Articles of Incorporation of the above-named

corporation. The purpose of said meeting is to adopt Bylaws, elect officers, and transact

such other business as may come before the meeting; and

Said organization meeting shall be held at _____

_____ on   , 19   , at   .m.

_____   _____

_____   _____

RECEIPT OF NOTICE

_____   _____
Address-Director   Date Received

NOTICE OF WAIVER OF
ANNUAL MEETING BY ALL SHAREHOLDERS

We, the undersigned, being the holders of all of the outstanding shares of stock of

, do hereby waive notice of the annual meeting of shareholders

scheduled to be held in the office of the Corporation at   ,

in the City of   , on   , 19   , at   .m.

The undersigned understand that the purposes of the meeting are to:

(1)   Elect a new board of directors.

(2)   Conduct any other business that properly may be brought before the
meeting.

Shareholder	Date	Number of Shares
_____	_____	_____
_____	_____	_____
_____	_____	_____

NOTICE TO DIRECTORS OF SPECIAL MEETING

Date:

A special meeting of the Board of Directors of   will be

held on   , 19   , at   .m., in the offices of the Corporation

located at   , in the City of   ,

to deliberate the following matter:

_____

Secretary

NOTICE TO SHAREHOLDERS OF SPECIAL MEETING

Date:

To the shareholders of   :

A special meeting of the shareholders of   will be

held on   , 19   , at   .m. in the offices of the Corporation

located at   .

Shareholders will be asked to deliberate and vote upon the following resolution

adopted by the Board of Directors:

The Board of Directors

of   Corporation

_____

Secretary

Only those shareholders who were shareholders of record at the close of business on

the   day of   , 19   , will be allowed to vote in person or by proxy at

the meeting or any adjournment thereof.

RESOLUTION:
CALL SHAREHOLDERS' MEETING

RESOLVED, that the annual meeting of shareholders of the corporation shall be held on

_____ , 19 ___ , at _____ .m. The meeting shall be held at the offices

of the Corporation located at _____ , in the

City of _____ , _____ .

The purpose of the meeting shall be:

(1) To elect a new board of directors.
(2) Transact such other business that may properly come before the meeting or any adjournment thereof.

Only shareholders who are shareholders of record on the _____ day of _____ ,

19 ___ , shall be entitled to vote at the meeting or any adjournment of the meeting.

The undersigned hereby certifies that he/she is the duly elected and qualified Secretary

and the custodian of the books and records and seal of _____ ,

a corporation duly formed pursuant to the laws of the State of _____ ,

and that the foregoing is a true record of a resolution duly adopted at a meeting of the

Board of Directors, and that said meeting was held in accordance with state law and the

Bylaws of the above-named Corporation on _____ , 19 ___ , and that said

resolution is now in full force and effect without modification or rescission.

IN WITNESS WHEREOF, I have executed my name as Secretary and have hereunto

affixed the corporate seal of the above-named Corporation this _____ day of _____ ,

19 ___ .

A True Record.

Attest.

_____
Secretary

(Seal)

RESOLUTION:
CHANGE DATE OF ANNUAL MEETING

WHEREAS, this Corporation wishes to change the date of the annual meeting, be it

RESOLVED, to change the date for the annual meeting of shareholders from   ,

19   , to   , 19   ; and that notice of said change of meeting date be duly

filed with the Division of Corporations, as required by the laws of the State of   .

The undersigned hereby certifies that he/she is the duly elected and qualified Secretary

and the custodian of the books and records and seal of   ,

a corporation duly formed pursuant to the laws of the State of   ,

and that the foregoing is a true record of a resolution duly adopted at a meeting of the

Stockholders, and that said meeting was held in accordance with state law and the Bylaws

of the above-named Corporation on   , 19   , and that said

resolution is now in full force and effect without modification or rescission.

IN WITNESS WHEREOF, I have executed my name as Secretary and have hereunto

affixed the corporate seal of the above-named Corporation this   day of   ,

19   .

A True Record.

Attest.

_____
Secretary

RESOLUTION:
FIX DATE FOR SHAREHOLDERS ELIGIBLE TO VOTE

WHEREAS, this corporation wishes to fix the date for shareholders to be eligible to vote, be it

RESOLVED, that the close of business on   , 19   , is hereby fixed as the time and date for determining shareholders who will be entitled to notice of and to the right to vote at at meeting of shareholders that will be held on the   day of   , 19   , in the City of   .

The undersigned hereby certifies that he/she is the duly elected and qualified Secretary and the custodian of the books and records and seal of   , a corporation duly formed pursuant to the laws of the State of   , and that the foregoing is a true record of a resolution duly adopted at a meeting of the Board of Directors, and that said meeting was held in accordance with state law and the Bylaws of the above-named Corporation on   , 19   , and that said resolution is now in full force and effect without modification or rescission.

IN WITNESS WHEREOF, I have executed my name as Secretary and have hereunto affixed the corporate seal of the above-named Corporation this   day of   , 19   .

A True Record.

Attest.

_____
Secretary

RESOLUTION:
SPECIAL MEETING TO ELECT DIRECTORS

WHEREAS, a board of directors was not elected at the last annual meeting of

shareholders, it is therefore

RESOLVED, that a special meeting of the shareholders of

Corporation shall be held on the   day of   , 19   , at   .m., at

the offices of the Corporation,   , in the

City of   , State of   ,

for the sole purpose of electing directors of the corporation.

The undersigned hereby certifies that he/she is the duly elected and qualified Secretary

and the custodian of the books and records and seal of   ,

a corporation duly formed pursuant to the laws of the State of   ,

and that the foregoing is a true record of a resolution duly adopted at a meeting of the

Board of Directors, and that said meeting was held in accordance with state law and the

Bylaws of the above-named Corporation on   , 19   , and that said

resolution is now in full force and effect without modification or rescission.

IN WITNESS WHEREOF, I have executed my name as Secretary and have hereunto

affixed the corporate seal of the above-named Corporation this   day of   ,

19   .

A True Record.

Attest.

_____
Secretary

RESOLUTION:
SPECIAL SHAREHOLDERS' MEETING

WHEREAS, the Board of Directors has adopted the following resolution:

RESOLVED, that a special meeting of the shareholders of the Corporation shall be held to deliberate said resolution. The special meeting shall be held at the offices of the Corporation, which are located at   , in the City of   , on   , 19   , at   .m.

The undersigned hereby certifies that he/she is the duly elected and qualified Secretary and the custodian of the books and records and seal of   ,
a corporation duly formed pursuant to the laws of the State of   ,
and that the foregoing is a true record of a resolution duly adopted at a meeting of the Board of Directors, and that said meeting was held in accordance with state law and the Bylaws of the above-named Corporation on   , 19   , and that said resolution is now in full force and effect without modification or rescission.

IN WITNESS WHEREOF, I have executed my name as Secretary and have hereunto affixed the corporate seal of the above-named Corporation this   day of   ,
19   .

A True Record.

Attest.

_____
Secretary

WAIVER OF NOTICE — COMBINED MEETING

I, the undersigned, the holder of   shares of stock of

and/or a Board of Director, do hereby waive notice of the combined meeting of

shareholders and board of directors of the said corporation.

Furthermore, the undersigned hereby agrees that said meeting shall be held at   .m.

on   , 19   , at the following location:

Date: _____

Shareholder/Director

WAIVER OF NOTICE OF ANNUAL MEETING
BY INDIVIDUAL SHAREHOLDER

I, the undersigned, the holder of   shares of stock of

                    , do hereby waive notice of the annual meeting of shareholders of the

                    Corporation which will be held for the following

purposes:

(1) Electing a new board of directors.

(2) Transacting any other business that may properly be brought before the meeting.

The undersigned hereby consents to the holding of the meeting on   ,

19   , at   .m. in the offices of the Corporation which are located at

                    , in the City of   .

Date: _____
                                         Shareholder

WAIVER OF NOTICE OF DIRECTORS' MEETING

The undersigned, constituting the entire membership of the Board of Directors of

_____, hereby waive notice of the meeting of the Board

of Directors of the Corporation and consent to the holding of the meeting at _____ .m.,

on _____ , 19____ , at the offices of the Corporation located at

_____ . Furthermore, we agree that any

lawful business may be transacted at the meeting.

Dated:

_____

_____

_____

WAIVER OF NOTICE OF ORGANIZATION
MEETING OF INCORPORATORS AND DIRECTORS
OF_____

We do hereby constitute the Incorporators and Directors of the above captioned

Corporation and do hereby waive notice of the organization meeting of Directors and

Incorporators of the said Corporation.

Furthermore, we hereby agree that said meeting shall be held at _____ .m. on

_____ , 19____ , at the following location: _____

_____ .

We do hereby affix our names to show our waiver of notice of said meeting.

_____   _____
Incorporator   Director

_____   _____
Incorporator   Director

Dated:

WRITTEN UNANIMOUS CONSENT IN LIEU OF A MEETING

The undersigned, being the holders of all of the outstanding shares of

Corporation entitled to vote at a meeting of shareholders, do hereby

consent to the following resolution adopted by the Board of Directors of

Corporation taken on   , 19   :

Signed:_____

_____

_____

Dated: , 19

Section Four
Stockholders' Forms

Form D401   Demands inspection of the corporation's books and records by a single shareholder.

Form I401   Authorizes another to attend a shareholders' meeting and vote on behalf of the shareholder. This authorization cannot be revoked and revokes all other previous authorizations.

Form L401   Lists shareholders of record as of the date established to be eligible to vote at the corporation's annual meeting.

Form P401   Authorizes another to attend a shareholders' meeting and vote on behalf of the shareholder.

Form R401   Revokes authorization to another to act as a proxy for shareholder.

Form S401   Is a request to issue a specific number of shares of the corporation to an individual upon payment of a specified sum.

DEMAND FOR INSPECTION OF
CORPORATE BOOKS AND RECORDS

The undersigned, _____ , is the holder of _____ shares of the common stock of _____ and does hereby demand the opportunity to inspect, at the office of the Corporation, the books and records of the Corporation, its stock ledger and the list of its shareholders. The undersigned does further state that the inspection is sought for a proper purpose, to wit:

The undersigned also states that he has never sold nor offered for sale any list of shareholders of any corporation, nor assisted any person in obtaining such a list or record for such purposes.

The requested date and time for inspection is:

Date: _____

Time: _____

State of
County of

On _____ before me, _____ ,
personally appeared _____ ,

who personally known to me (or proved to me on the basis of satisfactory evidence) to be the person(s) whose name(s) is/are subscribed to the within instrument and acknowledged to me that he/she/they executed the same in his/her/their authorized capacity(ies), and that by his/her/their signature(s) on the instrument the person(s), or the entity upon behalf of which the person(s) acted, executed the instrument.
WITNESS my hand and official seal.

Signature_____

My commission expires: _____

Affiant ____Known ____Produced ID
Type of ID _____

(Seal)

IRREVOCABLE PROXY

I, _____ , the holder of _____ shares of

the common voting stock of _____ Corporation, do

hereby irrevocably appoint _____ as my proxy to attend the

shareholders' meeting of _____ Corporation, to be held on

_____ , 19____ , or any continuations or adjournments of that meeting, with

full power to vote and act for me and in my name and place, in the same manner, and to

the same extent that I might act if I would have been in attendance at such meeting.

This proxy is irrevocable and has been issued to _____ who is a

pledgee holding a valid pledge of the shares owned by me. Any other proxy or proxies

previously given by me to others is hereby revoked.

Dated:

_____

State of
County of

On _____ before me, _____ ,
personally appeared

who personally known to me (or proved to me on the basis of satisfactory evidence) to be
the person(s) whose name(s) is/are subscribed to the within instrument and acknowledged
to me that he/she/they executed the same in his/her/their authorized capacity(ies), and
that by his/her/their signature(s) on the instrument the person(s), or the entity upon
behalf of which the person(s) acted, executed the instrument.
WITNESS my hand and official seal.
Signature_____
My commission expires: _____ Affiant ____Known
____Produced ID

Type of ID _____

(Seal)

LIST OF SHAREHOLDERS

I, _____ , Secretary of _____ Corporation,

hereby certify the following list of shareholders who own all outstanding stock of the

Corporation and who are entitled to vote at the shareholders' meeting on the

day of _____ , 19 ___ , because they were shareholders of record at the close of

business on the _____ day of _____ , 19 ___ .

Shareholder	Total Number of Shares Owned	Total Number of Voting Shares Owned
_____	_____	_____
_____	_____	_____
_____	_____	_____
_____	_____	_____

Dated:

_____
Secretary of the Corporation

PROXY TO VOTE SHARES

The undersigned, as owner of _____ shares of common voting stock in _____

_____ (Corporation), represented by Share Certificate No. _____ ,

hereby authorizes _____ to vote those shares at the meeting of

shareholders of the said Corporation to be held on the _____ day of _____ , 19 ___ , at

_____ .m., or any adjournment thereto, at _____ in the

City of _____ . Under this authority, _____ ,

shall have the right to vote for the election of directors and on any other matter as may

properly be raised at the meeting, all with the same force and effect as if I were voting said

shares personally.

_____

State of

County of

On _____ before me, _____ ,
personally appeared _____

who personally known to me (or proved to me on the basis of satisfactory evidence) to be
the person(s) whose name(s) is/are subscribed to the within instrument and acknowledged
to me that he/she/they executed the same in his/her/their authorized capacity(ies), and
that by his/her/their signature(s) on the instrument the person(s), or the entity upon
behalf of which the person(s) acted, executed the instrument.
WITNESS my hand and official seal.

Signature_____

My commission expires: _____   Affiant _____ Known _____ Produced ID

Type of ID _____

REVOCATION OF PROXY

I, _____ , the holder of _____ shares of

common voting stock of _____ (Corporation),

having appointed _____ to act as my proxy by a written

proxy dated _____ , 19 ___ , a copy of which is attached, do hereby revoke

that proxy.

IN WITNESS WHEREOF, I do hereby execute this revocation of proxy in duplicate on

this, the _____ day of _____ , 19 ___ . The original of this revocation shall be

filed in the office of _____ Corporation, and the

duplicate copy of this revocation shall be delivered by Certified Return Receipt mail, to

_____ , the person named by me as my proxy in the revoked

proxy agreement.

_____

State of
County of

On _____ before me, _____ ,
personally appeared

_____ ,

who personally known to me (or proved to me on the basis of satisfactory evidence) to be
the person(s) whose name(s) is/are subscribed to the within instrument and acknowledged
to me that he/she/they executed the same in his/her/their authorized capacity(ies), and
that by his/her/their signature(s) on the instrument the person(s), or the entity upon
behalf of which the person(s) acted, executed the instrument.
WITNESS my hand and official seal.

Signature_____
My commission expires: Affiant _____ Known _____ Produced ID
                                          Type of ID _____

(Seal)

STOCK SUBSCRIPTION

I,_____, the undersigned do hereby subscribe for

the purchase of   (   ) shares of the common stock of

_____ (Corporation) at $_____ per share, for the aggregate purchase

price of $_____. I understand that upon issue, said shares shall constitute   %

of the common shares outstanding and entitled to vote and that there are no other shares

outstanding.

_____
Subscriber

The foregoing subscription is accepted and the Treasurer shall issue said shares upon

payment to the corporation the sum of $_____.

_____
For the Corporation
and its Board of Directors

Section Five

Operations

Form R501   Authorizes the acquisition of the business assets of a specific business.

Form R502   Authorizes the acquisition of common stock of a specific business.

Form R503   Adopts a trade name the corporation will use for the conduct of certain business activities.

Form R504   Appoints a purchasing agent to make purchases on the corporation's behalf.

Form R505   Authorizes the corporation to implement a plan for Chapter 11 reorganization.

Form R506   Assigns corporation's lease to another party.

Form R507   Authorizes the appropriate corporate officers to execute a note to borrow a specific sum of money from a specific bank.

Form R508   Authorizes the corporation to enter a contract with a specific party for a specific purpose.

Form R509   Authorizes the corporation to become a franchisee.

Form R510   Authorizes repayment plan with creditors.

Form R511   Authorizes the sale of specific property to be leased back by the corporation.

Form R512   Grants the corporation's creditors a trust mortgage interest on its assets to secure a repayment plan.

Form R513   Gives the Board of Directors unlimited authority to sell the corporation's assets.

Form R514 Authorizes the corporation to borrow against its accounts receivable.

Form R515 Authorizes the corporation to borrow a specific sum from a specific officer or director and establishes repayment terms.

Form R516 Authorizes the corporation to borrow from a specific bank.

Form R517 Authorizes the corporation to borrow against its inventory and equipment.

Form R518 Authorizes the corporation to begin litigation and names counsel.

Form R519 Authorizes the corporation to transfer funds from the reserve for buildings to the surplus account.

Form R520 Authorizes the appropriate officer to defend the corporation against a lawsuit and retain an attorney.

Form R521 Authorizes the corporation to hire a specific person for a specific position at a specific salary.

Form R522 Exercises corporation's option to extend its lease.

Form R523 Authorizes the corporation to factor and assign to a specific party any and all of its accounts receivable.

Form R524 Authorizes the corporation to file for Chapter 11 reorganizatiaon.

Form R525 Authorizes the corporation to file for Chapter 7 bankruptcy.

Form R526 Authorizes the corporation to file for receivership.

Form R527 Grants a mortgage or security interest in the corporation's assets to obtain capital.

Form R528 Protects a party from any and all liability arising from a specific action.

Form R529 Gives corporate guarantee of a party's performance of a specific obligation.

Form R530	Grants an option to buy shares in the corporation to a specific party.
Form R531	Is a mutual release of any liability that may arise as a result of a specific act between the corporation and another party.
Form R532	Authorizes corporation to lease space to another party.
Form R533	Authorizes corporation to lease specific equipment from a specific party.
Form R534	Authorizes corporation to lease a specific motor vehicle from a specific party.
Form R535	Authorizes corporation to lease specific space from a specific party.
Form R536	Authorizes the corporation to loan money to an officer or director and establishes repayment terms.
Form R537	Assigns the corporation's assets to another for the benefit of creditors.
Form R538	Authorizes corporation to mortgage real estate to be held as collateral security for another obligation.
Form R539	Authorizes the appropriate officers of the corporation to negotiate a contract with a specific party for a specific purpose.
Form R540	Authorizes the corporation to apply for a corporate charge account.
Form R541	Authorizes the corporation to obtain appropriate licenses to conduct business.
Form R542	Authorizes the corporation to apply for a trademark for a specific product or service.
Form R543	Authorizes corporation to open bank and checking accounts.
Form R544	Authorizes corporation to purchase a boat for business purposes.
Form R545	Authorizes corporation to purchase equipment.

Form R546	Authorizes corporation to purchase a motor vehicle.
Form R547	Authorizes corporation to purchase real estate.
Form R548	Authorizes corporation to qualify as a foreign corporation.
Form R549	Ratifies and affirms actions of a specific officer by the corporation's Board of Directors.
Form R550	Ratifies and affirms actions of the Board of Directors by the shareholders.
Form R551	Authorizes the corporation to offer a redemption of shares to its stockholders.
Form R552	Reimburses expenses paid by a party in connection with the business of the Corporation.
Form R553	Retains an accountant for general accounting purposes, including the preparation of tax returns.
Form R554	Retains an attorney as the corporation's general counsel.
Form R555	Retains a business broker to sell corporation's business.
Form R556	Retains a consultant for specific assistance.
Form R557	Retains a real estate broker for purposes of selling certain real estate owned by the corporation.
Form R558	Retains a special accountant for a specific purpose.
Form R559	Retains a special attorney for a specific purpose.
Form R560	Authorizes the sale of corporate assets subject to shareholder approval.
Form R561	Accepts an offer to purchase the corporation's assets.
Form R562	Accepts a party's request to purchase a specific number of shares of the corporation.

Form R563	Authorizes sale of specific equipment owned by corporation.
Form R564	Authorizes sale of specifc motor vehicle owned by corporation.
Form R565	Authorizes sale of real estate owned by corporation.
Form R566	Authorizes settlement of claim.
Form R567	Authorizes corporation to sublet specific space.
Form R568	Terminates contract with another party.
Form R569	Terminates employee of corporation.
Form R570	Terminates lease as tenant.
Form R571	Waives retrictions on transfer of shares of stock of the corporation.

RESOLUTION:
ACQUIRE ASSETS OF BUSINESS

WHEREAS, it is considered advisable for the Corporation to purchase and acquire all or substantially all of the business assets of   , as a going business concern; be it

RESOLVED, that the Corporation execute an agreement to purchase the business assets of   , all in accordance with a purchase agreement annexed hereto; and be it

RESOLVED FURTHER, that the President of the Corporation be authorized to execute such further documents and undertake such other acts as are reasonably required to carry out and consummate said transaction to purchase assets.

RESOLVED, that the Board of Directors be and is authorized and empowered to take all actions necessary to sell and dispose of the assets and properties of the Corporation, all upon such price and terms as the Board in its discretion deems to be in the best interests of the Corporation.

The undersigned hereby certifies that he/she is the duly elected and qualified Secretary and the custodian of the books and records and seal of   ,

a corporation duly formed pursuant to the laws of the State of   ,

and that the foregoing is a true record of a resolution duly adopted at a meeting of the Stockholders, and that said meeting was held in accordance with state law and the Bylaws of the above-named Corporation on   , 19   , and that said resolution is now in full force and effect without modification or rescission.

IN WITNESS WHEREOF, I have executed my name as Secretary and have hereunto affixed the corporate seal of the above-named Corporation this   day of   ,

19   .

A True Record.

Attest.

_____
Secretary

RESOLUTION:
ACQUIRE SHARES OF STOCK

WHEREAS, the Board of Directors has determined that it is in the best interests of the Corporation to acquire certain shares of the common stock of

; be it

RESOLVED, that the Corporation acquire ( ) shares of the common stock of ; said shares representing

% of all shares, in all classes, outstanding, all for the aggregate purchase price of Dollars ($) per share, all as more particularly set forth in a stock purchase agreement as annexed hereto; and, be it

RESOLVED FURTHER, that the President and/or Treasurer of the Corporation undertake all actions necessary to carry out said resolution.

The undersigned hereby certifies that he/she is the duly elected and qualified Secretary and the custodian of the books and records and seal of ,

a corporation duly formed pursuant to the laws of the State of ,

and that the foregoing is a true record of a resolution duly adopted at a meeting of the Board of Directors, and that said meeting was held in accordance with state law and the Bylaws of the above-named Corporation on , 19 , and that said resolution is now in full force and effect without modification or rescission.

IN WITNESS WHEREOF, I have executed my name as Secretary and have hereunto affixed the corporate seal of the above-named Corporation this day of ,

19 .

A True Record.

Attest.

_____
Secretary

RESOLUTION:
ADOPT TRADE NAME

WHEREAS, it is desirous for the Corporation to adopt a trade name and style under which to conduct business; be it

RESOLVED, that the Corporation adopt the trade name:
as an assumed name for the conduct of certain business activities; and, be it

RESOLVED FURTHER, that the President of the Corporation record adoption and use of said fictitious name with the appropriate public records.

The undersigned hereby certifies that he/she is the duly elected and qualified Secretary and the custodian of the books and records and seal of   ,
a corporation duly formed pursuant to the laws of the State of   ,
and that the foregoing is a true record of a resolution duly adopted at a meeting of the Board of Directors, and that said meeting was held in accordance with state law and the Bylaws of the above-named Corporation on   , 19   , and that said resolution is now in full force and effect without modification or rescission.

IN WITNESS WHEREOF, I have executed my name as Secretary and have hereunto affixed the corporate seal of the above-named Corporation this   day of   ,
19   .

A True Record.

Attest.

_____
Secretary

RESOLUTION:
APPOINT A PURCHASING AGENT

WHEREAS, this Corporation wishes to appoint someone to be in charge of purchases for the Corportion, be it

RESOLVED, that   is hereby appointed Purchasing Agent of this Corporation with authority to make purchases in the Corporation's name and behalf. Under no circumstances is the Purchasing Agent to have authority to make a purchase for the Corporation if the dollar amount of the purchase or the total dollar amount of a purchase made in installments will exceed

dollars ($).

The undersigned hereby certifies that he/she is the duly elected and qualified Secretary and the custodian of the books and records and seal of   ,
a corporation duly formed pursuant to the laws of the State of   ,
and that the foregoing is a true record of a resolution duly adopted at a meeting of the Board of Directors, and that said meeting was held in accordance with state law and the Bylaws of the above-named Corporation on   , 19   , and that said resolution is now in full force and effect without modification or rescission.

IN WITNESS WHEREOF, I have executed my name as Secretary and have hereunto affixed the corporate seal of the above-named Corporation this   day of   ,
19   .

A True Record.

Attest.

_____
Secretary

RESOLUTION:
APPROVE CHAPTER 11 REORGANIZATION PLAN

WHEREAS, the Corporation has formulated a plan of reorganization that it believes is fair and feasible, and

WHEREAS, creditors of the Corporation have indicated support for said plans; be it

RESOLVED, that the Corporation affirms and approves the plan of reorganization under Chapter 11 of the Bankruptcy Code, all as set forth in the terms annexed hereto.

The undersigned hereby certifies that he/she is the duly elected and qualified Secretary and the custodian of the books and records and seal of   ,
a corporation duly formed pursuant to the laws of the State of   ,
and that the foregoing is a true record of a resolution duly adopted at a meeting of the Stockholders, and that said meeting was held in accordance with state law and the Bylaws of the above-named Corporation on   , 19   , and that said resolution is now in full force and effect without modification or rescission.

IN WITNESS WHEREOF, I have executed my name as Secretary and have hereunto affixed the corporate seal of the above-named Corporation this   day of   ,
19   .

A True Record.

Attest.

_____

Secretary

RESOLUTION:
ASSIGN LEASE

WHEREAS, the Corporation presently holds a lease for space that is no longer required for the conduct of the business; be it

RESOLVED, that the Corporation assign its lease for premises at

to   ; said lease assignment to be

effective   , 19   , and shall further be upon such terms and

conditions as are contained in a certain assignment of lease agreement annexed hereto.

The undersigned hereby certifies that he/she is the duly elected and qualified Secretary

and the custodian of the books and records and seal of   ,

a corporation duly formed pursuant to the laws of the State of   ,

and that the foregoing is a true record of a resolution duly adopted at a meeting of the

Board of Directors, and that said meeting was held in accordance with state law and the

Bylaws of the above-named Corporation on   , 19   , and that said

resolution is now in full force and effect without modification or rescission.

IN WITNESS WHEREOF, I have executed my name as Secretary and have hereunto

affixed the corporate seal of the above-named Corporation this   day of   ,

19   .

A True Record.

Attest.

_____
Secretary

RESOLUTION:
AUTHORIZE BORROWING ON LINE OF CREDIT

WHEREAS, this Company desires to borrow money, be it

RESOLVED, that the proper officers of this Company are hereby authorized to borrow

from the   Bank, for and in behalf of this Company, a sum

not to exceed   Dollars ($),

on its promissory note maturing   (   ) days from the date hereof, to

be signed by the proper officers of this Company, and to bear interest not to exceed the rate

of   percent (%) per annum, and with the additional privilege

of renewing the balance of said loan at its maturity, for another period of

(   ) days, and the proper officers of this Company are hereby authorized and

directed to sign any new or renewal note or notes required by said

Bank to carry out the provisions of this resolution, which new note or notes shall bear such

rate of interest as shall be agreed upon between this Company and the

Bank at the time of such renewal or renewals.

The undersigned hereby certifies that he/she is the duly elected and qualified Secretary

and the custodian of the books and records and seal of   ,

a corporation duly formed pursuant to the laws of the State of   ,

and that the foregoing is a true record of a resolution duly adopted at a meeting of the

Board of Directors, and that said meeting was held in accordance with state law and the

Bylaws of the above-named Corporation on   , 19   , and that said

resolution is now in full force and effect without modification or rescission.

IN WITNESS WHEREOF, I have executed my name as Secretary and have hereunto

affixed the corporate seal of the above-named Corporation this   day of   ,

19   .

A True Record.

Attest.

_____
Secretary

RESOLUTION:
AUTHORIZE CONTRACT

RESOLVED, that the Corporation enter into a contract with

for the general purposes of:

and all upon

such terms and conditions as are set forth in an agreement between the parties as annexed

hereto.

The undersigned hereby certifies that he/she is the duly elected and qualified Secretary

and the custodian of the books and records and seal of
,

a corporation duly formed pursuant to the laws of the State of
,

and that the foregoing is a true record of a resolution duly adopted at a meeting of the

Board of Directors, and that said meeting was held in accordance with state law and the

Bylaws of the above-named Corporation on   , 19   , and that said

resolution is now in full force and effect without modification or rescission.

IN WITNESS WHEREOF, I have executed my name as Secretary and have hereunto

affixed the corporate seal of the above-named Corporation this   day of   ,

19   .

A True Record.

Attest.

_____
Secretary

RESOLUTION:
AUTHORIZE FRANCHISE AGREEMENT

WHEREAS, the Corporation has the opportunity to become licensed as a franchisee of:

, and

WHEREAS, the Board of Directors of the Corporation has concluded that it would be in the best interest of the Corporation to operate as a licensed franchisee; be it

RESOLVED, that the Corporation enter into a franchise agreement with

, in accordance with the terms and conditions of a franchise agreement presented to and reviewed by the Board and as it is annexed hereto; and, be it

RESOLVED FURTHER, that the President of the Corporation undertake all actions as are necessary to perform the obligations of the Corporation under said agreement.

The undersigned hereby certifies that he/she is the duly elected and qualified Secretary and the custodian of the books and records and seal of   ,

a corporation duly formed pursuant to the laws of the State of   ,

and that the foregoing is a true record of a resolution duly adopted at a meeting of the Stockholders, and that said meeting was held in accordance with state law and the Bylaws of the above-named Corporation on   , 19   , and that said resolution is now in full force and effect without modification or rescission.

IN WITNESS WHEREOF, I have executed my name as Secretary and have hereunto affixed the corporate seal of the above-named Corporation this   day of   ,
19   .

A True Record.

Attest.

_____
Secretary

RESOLUTION:
AUTHORIZE REPAYMENT PLAN

WHEREAS, the Corporation is in arrears on certain obligations due creditors, and

WHEREAS, the Corporation is desirous of entering into a Repayment Plan with its creditors; be it

RESOLVED, that the Corporation hereby assents to a proposed composition agreement and plan of repayment with its creditors, all as contained in the draft agreement annexed hereto.

The undersigned hereby certifies that he/she is the duly elected and qualified Secretary and the custodian of the books and records and seal of   ,
a corporation duly formed pursuant to the laws of the State of   ,
and that the foregoing is a true record of a resolution duly adopted at a meeting of the Board of Directors, and that said meeting was held in accordance with state law and the Bylaws of the above-named Corporation on   , 19   , and that said resolution is now in full force and effect without modification or rescission.

IN WITNESS WHEREOF, I have executed my name as Secretary and have hereunto affixed the corporate seal of the above-named Corporation this   day of   ,
19   .

A True Record.

Attest.

                                                     _____

                                                     Secretary

RESOLUTION:
AUTHORIZE SALE/LEASEBACK

WHEREAS, it is advisable for the Corporation to raise capital through a sale/leaseback of certain of its assets; be it

RESOLVED, that the Corporation sell the following property:

to

for the price of $, and that concurrently the Corporation execute a lease

for said property for a period of years at a net annual rental not to exceed %

of the sales price, all in accord with generally prevailing sales/leaseback terms.

The undersigned hereby certifies that he/she is the duly elected and qualified Secretary

and the custodian of the books and records and seal of ,

a corporation duly formed pursuant to the laws of the State of ,

and that the foregoing is a true record of a resolution duly adopted at a meeting of the

Board of Directors, and that said meeting was held in accordance with state law and the

Bylaws of the above-named Corporation on , 19 , and that said

resolution is now in full force and effect without modification or rescission.

IN WITNESS WHEREOF, I have executed my name as Secretary and have hereunto

affixed the corporate seal of the above-named Corporation this day of ,

19 .

A True Record.

Attest.

_____
Secretary

RESOLUTION:
AUTHORIZE TRUST MORTGAGE

WHEREAS, the Corporation is in arrears on certain obligations due creditors, and

WHEREAS, the Corporation is desirous of entering into a repayment plan with its creditors, and securing said repayment obligation with a security interest on assets of the Corporation; be it

RESOLVED, that the Corporation grant to its assenting creditors a Trust Mortgage in accordance with the terms as set forth in the Trust Mortgage annexed hereto.

The undersigned hereby certifies that he/she is the duly elected and qualified Secretary and the custodian of the books and records and seal of   ,
a corporation duly formed pursuant to the laws of the State of   ,
and that the foregoing is a true record of a resolution duly adopted at a meeting of the Board of Directors, and that said meeting was held in accordance with state law and the Bylaws of the above-named Corporation on   , 19   , and that said resolution is now in full force and effect without modification or rescission.

IN WITNESS WHEREOF, I have executed my name as Secretary and have hereunto affixed the corporate seal of the above-named Corporation this   day of   ,
19   .

A True Record.

Attest.

_____
Secretary

RESOLUTION:
BLANKET AUTHORITY TO SELL ASSETS

RESOLVED, that the Board of Directors is hereby authorized to sell all or any part of the property and assets of this Corporation, including its good will, upon such terms and conditions and for such consideration as the Board of Directors shall deem in the best interests of the Corporation, and more especially, but without limitation of the foregoing, to sell its assets to:

The undersigned hereby certifies that he/she is the duly elected and qualified Secretary and the custodian of the books and records and seal of   ,

a corporation duly formed pursuant to the laws of the State of   ,

and that the foregoing is a true record of a resolution duly adopted at a meeting of the Stockholders, and that said meeting was held in accordance with state law and the Bylaws of the above-named Corporation on   , 19   , and that said resolution is now in full force and effect without modification or rescission.

IN WITNESS WHEREOF, I have executed my name as Secretary and have hereunto affixed the corporate seal of the above-named Corporation this   day of   ,

19   .

A True Record.

Attest.

_____
Secretary

RESOLUTION:
BORROW AGAINST ACCOUNTS RECEIVABLE

WHEREAS, the Corporation is or may be in need of additional operating funds; be it

RESOLVED, that the Corporation, through   , is hereby

authorized to borrow, from time to time, such sums as may be advisable or necessary for

the proper operation of the business, said borrowing to be upon such terms and conditions

as   may deem appropriate, and for that purpose the

Corporation may assign and pledge its accounts receivable as collateral security.

The undersigned hereby certifies that he/she is the duly elected and qualified Secretary

and the custodian of the books and records and seal of   ,

a corporation duly formed pursuant to the laws of the State of   ,

and that the foregoing is a true record of a resolution duly adopted at a meeting of the

Stockholders, and that said meeting was held in accordance with state law and the Bylaws

of the above-named Corporation on   , 19   , and that said

resolution is now in full force and effect without modification or rescission.

IN WITNESS WHEREOF, I have executed my name as Secretary and have hereunto

affixed the corporate seal of the above-named Corporation this   day of   ,

19   .

A True Record.

Attest.

_____

Secretary

RESOLUTION:
BORROW CAPITAL

WHEREAS, the Corporation is in need of additional capital, and

WHEREAS,   , as   of the

Corporation, has agreed to loan to the Corporation the sum of $, and

WHEREAS, such borrowing appears to be advantageous to the Corporation as it is on

better terms than would be available elsewhere; be it

RESOLVED, that the Corporation borrow the sum of $ from

                   , and that said sum be repaid in or within   years with

interest thereon at   % on the unpaid balance, all as more fully set forth in a

promissory note and collateral loan documents as have been presented to and reviewed by

this Board.

The undersigned hereby certifies that he/she is the duly elected and qualified Secretary

and the custodian of the books and records and seal of   ,

a corporation duly formed pursuant to the laws of the State of   ,

and that the foregoing is a true record of a resolution duly adopted at a meeting of the

Board of Directors, and that said meeting was held in accordance with state law and the

Bylaws of the above-named Corporation on   , 19   , and that said

resolution is now in full force and effect without modification or rescission.

IN WITNESS WHEREOF, I have executed my name as Secretary and have hereunto

affixed the corporate seal of the above-named Corporation this   day of   ,

19   .

A True Record.

Attest.

_____

Secretary

RESOLUTION:
BORROW FROM DESIGNATED BANK

RESOLVED, that the   of the Corporation is authorized, for the account of this Corporation, and on such terms and conditions as he/she may deem proper, to borrow from   (Bank) sums of money; and to sign, execute, and endorse all such documents as may be required by said bank to evidence such indebtedness; to discount or rediscount with said bank any of the bills receivable owned by this Corporation; to apply for and obtain from said bank letters of credit, and to execute agreements to secure said bank in connection therewith; to pledge and/or mortgage any moneys on deposit or any moneys otherwise in the possession of said band, and/or any bonds, stocks, receivables, or other property of this Corporation, to secure the payment of any indebtedness, liability, or obligation of this Corporation to said bank whether now due or to become due and whether existing or hereafter incurred, to withdraw and/or substitute any property held at any time by said bank as collateral, and to sign and execute trust receipts for the withdrawal of same when required; and generally to do and perform all acts and sign all agreements, obligations, pledges, and/or other instruments necessary or required by said bank.

The undersigned hereby certifies that he/she is the duly elected and qualified Secretary and the custodian of the books and records and seal of   , a corporation duly formed pursuant to the laws of the State of   , and that the foregoing is a true record of a resolution duly adopted at a meeting of the Board of Directors, and that said meeting was held in accordance with state law and the Bylaws of the above-named Corporation on   , 19   , and that said resolution is now in full force and effect without modification or rescission.

IN WITNESS WHEREOF, I have executed my name as Secretary and have hereunto affixed the corporate seal of the above-named Corporation this   day of   , 19   .

A True Record.

Attest.

_____
Secretary

RESOLUTION:
BORROW ON INVENTORY AND EQUIPMENT

WHEREAS, this Corporation wishes to borrow for corporate purposes, be it

RESOLVED, that   , the President of this

Corporation, is hereby authorized and directed to borrow the sum of

Dollars ($) from

on the terms set out in the Promissory Note attached to the minutes of this meeting and to

execute a mortgage in favor of the Lender covering the furniture, fixtures and inventory of

merchandise set out in the Schedule attached to the minutes of this meeting, and it is

FURTHER RESOLVED, that the President of the Corporation is hereby authorized and

directed to provide for creditors of the Corporation all notices required by law to be given

to the creditors of the Corporation, and to do everything else that may be necessary to

complete the authorized transaction.

The undersigned hereby certifies that he/she is the duly elected and qualified Secretary

and the custodian of the books and records and seal of   ,

a corporation duly formed pursuant to the laws of the State of   ,

and that the foregoing is a true record of a resolution duly adopted at a meeting of the

Stockholders, and that said meeting was held in accordance with state law and the Bylaws

of the above-named Corporation on   , 19   , and that said

resolution is now in full force and effect without modification or rescission.

IN WITNESS WHEREOF, I have executed my name as Secretary and have hereunto

affixed the corporate seal of the above-named Corporation this   day of   ,

19   .

A True Record.

Attest.

_____
Secretary

RESOLUTION:
COMMENCE LITIGATION

WHEREAS, based on advice of counsel, the Corporation believes it has a valid claim

against   summarily arising from

                                      , be it

RESOLVED, that the Corporation pursue its claim, through court proceedings, if

necessary; and that it be

FURTHER RESOLVED, that   act as counsel for the

Corporation on said matter upon such fee arrangement as may be customarily prevailing

and agreeable to the President of the Corporation; and that it be

FURTHER RESOLVED, that the President of the Corporation, upon the

recommendation of counsel, be authorized to settle said claim for such amount and on

such terms as the President deems to be in the best interests of the Corporation.

The undersigned hereby certifies that he/she is the duly elected and qualified Secretary

and the custodian of the books and records and seal of   ,

a corporation duly formed pursuant to the laws of the State of   ,

and that the foregoing is a true record of a resolution duly adopted at a meeting of the

Board of Directors, and that said meeting was held in accordance with state law and the

Bylaws of the above-named Corporation on   , 19   , and that said

resolution is now in full force and effect without modification or rescission.

IN WITNESS WHEREOF, I have executed my name as Secretary and have hereunto

affixed the corporate seal of the above-named Corporation this   day of   ,

19   .

A True Record.

Attest.

_____
Secretary

RESOLUTION:
CONVERT EXCESS DEPRECIATION TO SURPLUS

WHEREAS   dollars ($)

has been assigned to the depreciation account on the Corporation's books for the period

running from   , 19   , to   , 19   , and

WHEREAS   dollars ($)

has been assigned to the reserve for depreciation on the books of the Corporation, and

WHEREAS the value of the real property upon which said depreciation and reserve for

depreciation charges and credits were made has been determined to be

            dollars ($), it is hereby

RESOLVED that the Treasurer of this Corporation is hereby authorized and directed to

transfer on the Corporation's books

dollars ($) from the Corporation's reserve for buildings account to the

Corporation's surplus account.

The undersigned hereby certifies that he/she is the duly elected and qualified Secretary

and the custodian of the books and records and seal of   ,

a corporation duly formed pursuant to the laws of the State of   ,

and that the foregoing is a true record of a resolution duly adopted at a meeting of the

Board of Directors, and that said meeting was held in accordance with state law and the

Bylaws of the above-named Corporation on   , 19   , and that said

resolution is now in full force and effect without modification or rescission.

IN WITNESS WHEREOF, I have executed my name as Secretary and have hereunto

affixed the corporate seal of the above-named Corporation this   day of   ,

19   .

A True Record.

Attest.

_____
Secretary

RESOLUTION:
DEFEND SUIT

WHEREAS, a claim has been made by   against the

Corporation, which claim summarily asserts:

                                                                              , and

WHEREAS, it is believed that the Corporation has a valid and good defense against

said claim; it is

RESOLVED, that the Corporation defend against said claim; and it is

RESOLVED, that the Corporation retain   as attorneys to

defend said action; and

RESOLVED FURTHER, that the President, upon the recommendation of counsel, be

authorized to compromise and settle said claim for an amount and on such terms as

deemed to be in the best interests of the Corporation.

The undersigned hereby certifies that he/she is the duly elected and qualified Secretary

and the custodian of the books and records and seal of   ,

a corporation duly formed pursuant to the laws of the State of   ,

and that the foregoing is a true record of a resolution duly adopted at a meeting of the

Board of Directors, and that said meeting was held in accordance with state law and the

Bylaws of the above-named Corporation on   , 19   , and that said

resolution is now in full force and effect without modification or rescission.

IN WITNESS WHEREOF, I have executed my name as Secretary and have hereunto

affixed the corporate seal of the above-named Corporation this   day of   ,

19   .

A True Record.

Attest.

_____

Secretary

RESOLUTION:
EMPLOY

WHEREAS, the Corporation is in need of a   , and

WHEREAS,   has applied for said position and appears well qualified to perform the duties required of said position; be it

RESOLVED, that the Corporation offer   a contract of employment to serve in the capacity of   , at a salary not to exceed $ per year, together with the customary benefits appertaining thereto.

The undersigned hereby certifies that he/she is the duly elected and qualified Secretary and the custodian of the books and records and seal of   , a corporation duly formed pursuant to the laws of the State of   , and that the foregoing is a true record of a resolution duly adopted at a meeting of the Board of Directors, and that said meeting was held in accordance with state law and the Bylaws of the above-named Corporation on   , 19   , and that said resolution is now in full force and effect without modification or rescission.

IN WITNESS WHEREOF, I have executed my name as Secretary and have hereunto affixed the corporate seal of the above-named Corporation this   day of   , 19   .

A True Record.

Attest.

_____
Secretary

RESOLUTION:
EXERCISE OPTION TO EXTEND LEASE

WHEREAS, the Corporation presently holds a lease due to expire, and

WHEREAS, it is in the best interests of the Corporation to exercise its option to extend the lease; be it

RESOLVED, that the Corporation exercise its option to extend a lease which it holds as tenant from   , as landlord, said lease dated

                    , 19   , for premises at

.

The undersigned hereby certifies that he/she is the duly elected and qualified Secretary and the custodian of the books and records and seal of   ,
a corporation duly formed pursuant to the laws of the State of   ,
and that the foregoing is a true record of a resolution duly adopted at a meeting of the Board of Directors, and that said meeting was held in accordance with state law and the Bylaws of the above-named Corporation on   , 19   , and that said resolution is now in full force and effect without modification or rescission.

IN WITNESS WHEREOF, I have executed my name as Secretary and have hereunto affixed the corporate seal of the above-named Corporation this   day of   ,
19   .

A True Record.

Attest.

_____
Secretary

RESOLUTION:
FACTOR ACCOUNTS RECEIVABLE

WHEREAS, it is advisable for the Corporation to raise capital, and

WHEREAS, it is in the best interests of the Corporation to raise said capital through factoring of its accounts receivable; be it

RESOLVED, to factor and assign from time to time all or any part of the accounts receivable of the Corporation to   , pursuant to the terms of a factoring agreement as annexed hereto.

The undersigned hereby certifies that he/she is the duly elected and qualified Secretary and the custodian of the books and records and seal of   , a corporation duly formed pursuant to the laws of the State of   , and that the foregoing is a true record of a resolution duly adopted at a meeting of the Board of Directors, and that said meeting was held in accordance with state law and the Bylaws of the above-named Corporation on   , 19   , and that said resolution is now in full force and effect without modification or rescission.

IN WITNESS WHEREOF, I have executed my name as Secretary and have hereunto affixed the corporate seal of the above-named Corporation this   day of   ,
19   .

A True Record.

Attest.

_____
Secretary

RESOLUTION:
FILE CHAPTER 11 REORGANIZATION

WHEREAS, the Corporation is insolvent and unable to pay its debts when due, and

WHEREAS, the Corporation and its creditors would best be served by reorganization of the Corporation under Chapter 11 of the Bankruptcy Code; be it

RESOLVED, that the Corporation file as soon as practicable for reorganization pursuant to Chapter 11 of the Bankruptcy Code.

The undersigned hereby certifies that he/she is the duly elected and qualified Secretary and the custodian of the books and records and seal of   ,

a corporation duly formed pursuant to the laws of the State of   ,

and that the foregoing is a true record of a resolution duly adopted at a meeting of the

Stockholders, and that said meeting was held in accordance with state law and the Bylaws

of the above-named Corporation on   , 19   , and that said

resolution is now in full force and effect without modification or rescission.

IN WITNESS WHEREOF, I have executed my name as Secretary and have hereunto

affixed the corporate seal of the above-named Corporation this   day of   ,

19   .

A True Record.

Attest.

_____

Secretary

RESOLUTION:
FILE CHAPTER 7 BANKRUPTCY

WHEREAS, the Corporation is insolvent and unable to pay its debts as they mature, and

WHEREAS, it would be in the best interests of creditors for the Corporation to file a voluntary petition under Chapter 7 of the Bankruptcy Code; it is

RESOLVED, that the Corporation file as soon as practicable a bankruptcy in accordance with Chapter 7 of the Bankruptcy Code.

The undersigned hereby certifies that he/she is the duly elected and qualified Secretary and the custodian of the books and records and seal of   ,

a corporation duly formed pursuant to the laws of the State of   ,

and that the foregoing is a true record of a resolution duly adopted at a meeting of the Stockholders, and that said meeting was held in accordance with state law and the Bylaws of the above-named Corporation on   , 19   , and that said resolution is now in full force and effect without modification or rescission.

IN WITNESS WHEREOF, I have executed my name as Secretary and have hereunto affixed the corporate seal of the above-named Corporation this   day of   ,

19   .

A True Record.

Attest.

_____
Secretary

RESOLUTION:
FILE FOR RECEIVERSHIP

WHEREAS, the Corporation is insolvent and unable to pay its debts as they become due, and

WHEREAS, it would be in the best interests of creditors to liquidate the assets of the business pursuant to receivership; be it

RESOLVED, that the Corporation file as soon as practicable a petition for receivership in accordance with state laws.

The undersigned hereby certifies that he/she is the duly elected and qualified Secretary and the custodian of the books and records and seal of   ,
a corporation duly formed pursuant to the laws of the State of   ,
and that the foregoing is a true record of a resolution duly adopted at a meeting of the Stockholders, and that said meeting was held in accordance with state law and the Bylaws of the above-named Corporation on   , 19   , and that said resolution is now in full force and effect without modification or rescission.

IN WITNESS WHEREOF, I have executed my name as Secretary and have hereunto affixed the corporate seal of the above-named Corporation this   day of   ,
19   .

A True Record.

Attest.

_____
Secretary

RESOLUTION:
GRANT MORTGAGE/SECURITY INTEREST

WHEREAS, the Board of Directors has deemed it in the best interests of the

Corporation to undertake certain obligations generally referred to:

, and

WHEREAS, it is required that the Corporation pledge certain collateral as security for

said obligation; be it

RESOLVED, that the Corporation grant a mortgage or security interest on assets of the

Corporation listed and described as:

, and

RESOLVED FURTHER, that the President and/or Treasurer execute and deliver all

mortgages, security agreements, loan documents and such related agreements as they

deem necessary to secure said obligation as is provided for herein.

The undersigned hereby certifies that he/she is the duly elected and qualified Secretary

and the custodian of the books and records and seal of   ,

a corporation duly formed pursuant to the laws of the State of   ,

and that the foregoing is a true record of a resolution duly adopted at a meeting of the

Stockholders, and that said meeting was held in accordance with state law and the Bylaws

of the above-named Corporation on   , 19   , and that said

resolution is now in full force and effect without modification or rescission.

IN WITNESS WHEREOF, I have executed my name as Secretary and have hereunto

affixed the corporate seal of the above-named Corporation this   day of   ,

19   .

A True Record.

Attest.

_____

Secretary

RESOLUTION:
INDEMNIFY AND SAVE HARMLESS

RESOLVED, that the Corporation indemnify and save harmless

and his or her successors and assigns from any and all liability

arising from:

Said indemnification being upon such terms as are contained in an indemnification

agreement annexed hereto.

The undersigned hereby certifies that he/she is the duly elected and qualified Secretary

and the custodian of the books and records and seal of   ,

a corporation duly formed pursuant to the laws of the State of   ,

and that the foregoing is a true record of a resolution duly adopted at a meeting of the

Board of Directors, and that said meeting was held in accordance with state law and the

Bylaws of the above-named Corporation on   , 19   , and that said

resolution is now in full force and effect without modification or rescission.

IN WITNESS WHEREOF, I have executed my name as Secretary and have hereunto

affixed the corporate seal of the above-named Corporation this   day of   ,

19   .

A True Record.

Attest.

_____
Secretary

RESOLUTION:
ISSUE GUARANTEE

WHEREAS,   is or shall be indebted to

on an obligation described as: ,

and

WHEREAS, it has been requested that the Corporation issue its guaranty to the

performance of   under said obligation, and

WHEREAS, it is in the best interest of the Corporation to extend its guaranty as

aforesaid; be it

RESOLVED, that the Corporation guarantee the performance of

under said above obligation and that the Corporation execute and deliver the

guaranty as annexed hereto.

The undersigned hereby certifies that he/she is the duly elected and qualified Secretary

and the custodian of the books and records and seal of   ,

a corporation duly formed pursuant to the laws of the State of   ,

and that the foregoing is a true record of a resolution duly adopted at a meeting of the

Board of Directors, and that said meeting was held in accordance with state law and the

Bylaws of the above-named Corporation on   , 19   , and that said

resolution is now in full force and effect without modification or rescission.

IN WITNESS WHEREOF, I have executed my name as Secretary and have hereunto

affixed the corporate seal of the above-named Corporation this   day of   ,

19   .

A True Record.

Attest.

_____
Secretary

RESOLUTION:
ISSUE OPTION TO BUY SHARES

WHEREAS, in the judgment of the Board of Directors, it is in the best interests of the

Corporation to grant to   an option to purchase

a certain number of shares of common stock of the Corporation; be it

RESOLVED, that for the good consideration, the Corporation grant and issue to

an option to purchase an aggregate of (   ) shares

of the unissued common stock of the Corporation for the option price of $

per share. This option shall terminate on   , 19   .

The undersigned hereby certifies that he/she is the duly elected and qualified Secretary

and the custodian of the books and records and seal of   ,

a corporation duly formed pursuant to the laws of the State of   ,

and that the foregoing is a true record of a resolution duly adopted at a meeting of the

Stockholders, and that said meeting was held in accordance with state law and the Bylaws

of the above-named Corporation on   , 19   , and that said

resolution is now in full force and effect without modification or rescission.

IN WITNESS WHEREOF, I have executed my name as Secretary and have hereunto

affixed the corporate seal of the above-named Corporation this   day of   ,

19   .

A True Record.

Attest.

_____
Secretary

RESOLUTION:
ISSUE RELEASE

WHEREAS, a claim has or may arise between the Corporation and

, arising from:

; be it

RESOLVED, that to terminate any possibility of future claim by or against the

Corporation arising from the above, that the Corporation execute and deliver a general

release to the said   , provided the Corporation and its

agents, employees, successors and assigns are simultaneously released by a release signed

by   .

The undersigned hereby certifies that he/she is the duly elected and qualified Secretary

and the custodian of the books and records and seal of   ,

a corporation duly formed pursuant to the laws of the State of   ,

and that the foregoing is a true record of a resolution duly adopted at a meeting of the

Board of Directors, and that said meeting was held in accordance with state law and the

Bylaws of the above-named Corporation on   , 19   , and that said

resolution is now in full force and effect without modification or rescission.

IN WITNESS WHEREOF, I have executed my name as Secretary and have hereunto

affixed the corporate seal of the above-named Corporation this   day of   ,

19   .

A True Record.

Attest.

_____
Secretary

RESOLUTION:
LEASE AS LESSOR

WHEREAS, the Corporation has available certain space for rental; be it

RESOLVED, that the Corporation, as lessor, lease certain space known as

to   ,

as lessee; said lease being upon the terms and conditions of a certain lease as annexed

hereto.

The undersigned hereby certifies that he/she is the duly elected and qualified Secretary

and the custodian of the books and records and seal of   ,

a corporation duly formed pursuant to the laws of the State of   ,

and that the foregoing is a true record of a resolution duly adopted at a meeting of the

Board of Directors, and that said meeting was held in accordance with state law and the

Bylaws of the above-named Corporation on   , 19   , and that said

resolution is now in full force and effect without modification or rescission.

IN WITNESS WHEREOF, I have executed my name as Secretary and have hereunto

affixed the corporate seal of the above-named Corporation this   day of   ,

19   .

A True Record.

Attest.

_____

Secretary

RESOLUTION:
LEASE EQUIPMENT

WHEREAS, it is necessary to the efficient operation of the business to obtain certain additional equipment; and

WHEREAS, it is more advantageous to the Corporation to lease rather than buy; be it

RESOLVED, to lease certain equipment generally described as

_____ from _____, all in accordance with the terms of a certain lease agreement annexed hereto.

The undersigned hereby certifies that he/she is the duly elected and qualified Secretary and the custodian of the books and records and seal of _____, a corporation duly formed pursuant to the laws of the State of _____ and that the foregoing is a true record of a resolution duly adopted at a meeting of the Board of Directors, and that said meeting was held in accordance with state law and the Bylaws of the above-named Corporation on _____, 19___, and that said resolution is now in full force and effect without modification or rescission.

IN WITNESS WHEREOF, I have executed my name as Secretary and have hereunto affixed the corporate seal of the above-named Corporation this ___ day of _____, 19___.

A True Record.

Attest.

_____
Secretary

RESOLUTION:
LEASE MOTOR VEHICLES

WHEREAS, the Corporation has need for an additional motor vehicle, and

WHEREAS, it is more advantageous to the Corporation to lease rather than buy said vehicle; be it

RESOLVED, to lease a motor vehicle described as   ,
from   , pursuant to the terms of a lease agreement as annexed hereto.

The undersigned hereby certifies that he/she is the duly elected and qualified Secretary and the custodian of the books and records and seal of   ,
a corporation duly formed pursuant to the laws of the State of   ,
and that the foregoing is a true record of a resolution duly adopted at a meeting of the Board of Directors, and that said meeting was held in accordance with state law and the Bylaws of the above-named Corporation on   , 19   , and that said resolution is now in full force and effect without modification or rescission.

IN WITNESS WHEREOF, I have executed my name as Secretary and have hereunto affixed the corporate seal of the above-named Corporation this   day of   ,
19   .

A True Record.

Attest.

_____
Secretary

RESOLUTION:
LEASE PREMISES

WHEREAS, the Corporation has certain space requirements as is necessary for the efficient operation of the business; be it

RESOLVED, that the Corporation accept as tenant, a lease from

, as landlord, the premises known as

, in accordance with the terms and conditions of a certain lease as annexed.

The undersigned hereby certifies that he/she is the duly elected and qualified Secretary and the custodian of the books and records and seal of   ,
a corporation duly formed pursuant to the laws of the State of   ,
and that the foregoing is a true record of a resolution duly adopted at a meeting of the Board of Directors, and that said meeting was held in accordance with state law and the Bylaws of the above-named Corporation on   , 19   , and that said resolution is now in full force and effect without modification or rescission.

IN WITNESS WHEREOF, I have executed my name as Secretary and have hereunto affixed the corporate seal of the above-named Corporation this   day of   ,
19   .

A True Record.

Attest.

_____
Secretary

RESOLUTION:
LOAN FUNDS

WHEREAS, _____ , a _____ of this

Corporation, has requested of this Corporation an advance and loan in the amount of

$ _____ together with interest, and

WHEREAS, the Corporation has adequate financial resources to make such loan

without impairing its growth or profitability, and that said loan is deemed reasonably

secure and in the best interests of the Corporation to make; be it

RESOLVED, that the Corporation issue a loan to _____ , in the amount

of $ _____ , to be repaid within _____ months with interest of _____ % on the unpaid

balance, and that the borrower execute to the Corporation promissory notes evidencing

said indebtedness.

The undersigned hereby certifies that he/she is the duly elected and qualified Secretary

and the custodian of the books and records and seal of _____ ,

a corporation duly formed pursuant to the laws of the State of _____ ,

and that the foregoing is a true record of a resolution duly adopted at a meeting of the

Board of Directors, and that said meeting was held in accordance with state law and the

Bylaws of the above-named Corporation on _____ , 19 _____ , and that said

resolution is now in full force and effect without modification or rescission.

IN WITNESS WHEREOF, I have executed my name as Secretary and have hereunto

affixed the corporate seal of the above-named Corporation this _____ day of _____ ,

19 _____ .

A True Record.

Attest.

_____
Secretary

RESOLUTION:
MAKE ASSIGNMENT FOR BENEFIT OF CREDITORS

WHEREAS, the Corporation is insolvent and indebted to numerous creditors, and

WHEREAS, it is in the best interests of creditors as well as the Corporation to liquidate the assets of the Corporation through an assignment for the benefit of creditors; be it

RESOLVED, that the Corporation make a general assignment for the benefit of creditors, naming   as assignee.

The undersigned hereby certifies that he/she is the duly elected and qualified Secretary and the custodian of the books and records and seal of   ,
a corporation duly formed pursuant to the laws of the State of   ,
and that the foregoing is a true record of a resolution duly adopted at a meeting of the Board of Directors, and that said meeting was held in accordance with state law and the Bylaws of the above-named Corporation on   , 19   , and that said resolution is now in full force and effect without modification or rescission.

IN WITNESS WHEREOF, I have executed my name as Secretary and have hereunto affixed the corporate seal of the above-named Corporation this   day of   ,
19   .

A True Record.

Attest.

_____
Secretary

RESOLUTION:
MORTGAGE REAL ESTATE

RESOLVED, that the Corporation grant to   a

mortgage on certain real estate known or described as

, and that said mortgage shall be collateral security for a

certain obligation as contained in the documents annexed hereto.

The undersigned hereby certifies that he/she is the duly elected and qualified Secretary

and the custodian of the books and records and seal of

,

a corporation duly formed pursuant to the laws of the State of

,

and that the foregoing is a true record of a resolution duly adopted at a meeting of the

Board of Directors, and that said meeting was held in accordance with state law and the

Bylaws of the above-named Corporation on   , 19   , and that said

resolution is now in full force and effect without modification or rescission.

IN WITNESS WHEREOF, I have executed my name as Secretary and have hereunto

affixed the corporate seal of the above-named Corporation this   day of   ,

19   .

A True Record.

Attest.

_____
Secretary

RESOLUTION:
NEGOTIATE CONTRACT

RESOLVED, that the President of this Corporation be hereby authorized and empowered to enter into a contract for

with , in the

name and in behalf of this Corporation, upon such terms and conditions as may be agreed

upon, at the sole discretion of said officer.

The undersigned hereby certifies that he/she is the duly elected and qualified Secretary

and the custodian of the books and records and seal of ,

a corporation duly formed pursuant to the laws of the State of ,

and that the foregoing is a true record of a resolution duly adopted at a meeting of the

Board of Directors, and that said meeting was held in accordance with state law and the

Bylaws of the above-named Corporation on , 19 , and that said

resolution is now in full force and effect without modification or rescission.

IN WITNESS WHEREOF, I have executed my name as Secretary and have hereunto

affixed the corporate seal of the above-named Corporation this day of ,

19 .

A True Record.

Attest.

_____
Secretary

RESOLUTION:
OBTAIN CORPORATE CHARGE CARD

WHEREAS, it is advisable to obtain charge card privileges for purposes of charging

certain expenses relative to the business affairs of the Corporation; be it

RESOLVED, that _____ , as President of the

Corporation, apply for and obtain a Corporate Charge Card from

with such credit limit as the president deems advisable, and that

NAME	TITLE
_____	_____
_____	_____
_____	_____
_____	_____

be authorized to charge on that account any travel, entertainment and other expenses that

are reasonably related to carrying out the business of the Corporation as provided for by

the Internal Revenue Code, and that the Treasurer of the Corporation is directed to monitor

said account and pay such proper charges as they fall due.

The undersigned hereby certifies that he/she is the duly elected and qualified Secretary

and the custodian of the books and records and seal of   ,

a corporation duly formed pursuant to the laws of the State of   ,

and that the foregoing is a true record of a resolution duly adopted at a meeting of the

Board of Directors, and that said meeting was held in accordance with state law and the Bylaws of the above-named Corporation on   , 19   , and that said resolution is now in full force and effect without modification or rescission.

IN WITNESS WHEREOF, I have executed my name as Secretary and have hereunto affixed the corporate seal of the above-named Corporation this   day of   , 19   .

A True Record.

Attest.

_____
Secretary

RESOLUTION:
OBTAIN LICENSE

WHEREAS, the Corporation requires certain licenses and permits for the lawful conduct of the activity generally described as:

; be it

RESOLVED, that the Corporation apply to the appropriate governmental agency for such requisite licenses and permits which shall include but not necessarily be limited to:

The undersigned hereby certifies that he/she is the duly elected and qualified Secretary and the custodian of the books and records and seal of

a corporation duly formed pursuant to the laws of the State of

and that the foregoing is a true record of a resolution duly adopted at a meeting of the Board of Directors, and that said meeting was held in accordance with state law and the Bylaws of the above-named Corporation on   , 19   , and that said resolution is now in full force and effect without modification or rescission.

IN WITNESS WHEREOF, I have executed my name as Secretary and have hereunto affixed the corporate seal of the above-named Corporation this   day of   ,
19   .

A True Record.

Attest.

_____
Secretary

RESOLUTION:
OBTAIN TRADEMARK

WHEREAS, the Corporation has adopted the name

as our identifying mark for the product/service

, and

WHEREAS, the Corporation desires to secure the exclusive rights to said name and/or

mark; be it

RESOLVED, that the Corporation apply to the United States Patent Office for a

trademark/service on:

and that the Corporation undertake all action necessary to successfully obtain and enforce

its trademark application.

The undersigned hereby certifies that he/she is the duly elected and qualified Secretary

and the custodian of the books and records and seal of   ,

a corporation duly formed pursuant to the laws of the State of   ,

and that the foregoing is a true record of a resolution duly adopted at a meeting of the

Board of Directors, and that said meeting was held in accordance with state law and the

Bylaws of the above-named Corporation on   , 19   , and that said

resolution is now in full force and effect without modification or rescission.

IN WITNESS WHEREOF, I have executed my name as Secretary and have hereunto

affixed the corporate seal of the above-named Corporation this   day of   ,

19   .

A True Record.

Attest.

_____
                           Secretary

RESOLUTION:
OPEN BANK/CHECKING ACCOUNTS

WHEREAS, the Board of Directors has determined it to be in the best interest of the

Corporation to establish a banking resolution with

bank; be it

RESOLVED, that the Corporation execute and deliver to said bank a duly signed

original of the completed banking resolution as is annexed hereto, and that the authority to

transact business — including but not limited to the maintenance of savings, checking and

other accounts as well as borrowing by the Corporation — shall be as contained in said

resolution with the named officers therein authorized to so act on behalf of the Corporation

as specified thereto.

The undersigned hereby certifies that he/she is the duly elected and qualified Secretary

and the custodian of the books and records and seal of
,

a corporation duly formed pursuant to the laws of the State of
,

and that the foregoing is a true record of a resolution duly adopted at a meeting of the

Stockholders, and that said meeting was held in accordance with state law and the Bylaws

of the above-named Corporation on   , 19   , and that said

resolution is now in full force and effect without modification or rescission.

IN WITNESS WHEREOF, I have executed my name as Secretary and have hereunto

affixed the corporate seal of the above-named Corporation this   day of   ,

19   .

A True Record.

Attest.

_____
Secretary

RESOLUTION:
PURCHASE BOAT

WHEREAS, the Board of Directors has determined it to be in the best interests of the Corporation to purchase a boat for purposes of entertaining customers and prospective customers of the Corporation; be it

RESOLVED, that the Corporation purchase a boat on the following specifications:

Year:

Make:

Model:

Length:

Price:

; and, be it

RESOLVED FURTHER, that the President and/or Treasurer of the Corporation maintain accurate records to document use of the boat for legitimate business purposes, and they are further authorized to pay all incidental costs of dockage, storage, insurance, maintenance and repair as is reasonably required to safekeep the value of said boat.

The undersigned hereby certifies that he/she is the duly elected and qualified Secretary and the custodian of the books and records and seal of   ,

a corporation duly formed pursuant to the laws of the State of   , and that the foregoing is a true record of a resolution duly adopted at a meeting of the Stockholders, and that said meeting was held in accordance with state law and the Bylaws of the above-named Corporation on   , 19   , and that said resolution is now in full force and effect without modification or rescission.

IN WITNESS WHEREOF, I have executed my name as Secretary and have hereunto affixed the corporate seal of the above-named Corporation this   day of   , 19   .

A True Record.

Attest.

_____
Secretary

RESOLUTION:
PURCHASE EQUIPMENT

WHEREAS, it is necessary to purchase certain additional equipment for the efficient operation of the business; be it

RESOLVED, to purchase certain equipment described generally as

from   for the purchase price

of $.

The undersigned hereby certifies that he/she is the duly elected and qualified Secretary

and the custodian of the books and records and seal of   ,

a corporation duly formed pursuant to the laws of the State of   ,

and that the foregoing is a true record of a resolution duly adopted at a meeting of the

Board of Directors, and that said meeting was held in accordance with state law and the

Bylaws of the above-named Corporation on   , 19   , and that said

resolution is now in full force and effect without modification or rescission.

IN WITNESS WHEREOF, I have executed my name as Secretary and have hereunto

affixed the corporate seal of the above-named Corporation this   day of   ,

19   .

A True Record.

Attest.

_____
Secretary

RESOLUTION:
PURCHASE MOTOR VEHICLE

WHEREAS, an additional motor vehicle is necessary for the operation of the business; be it

RESOLVED, to purchase a motor vehicle described as

from   for the purchase price

of $.

The undersigned hereby certifies that he/she is the duly elected and qualified Secretary

and the custodian of the books and records and seal of   ,

a corporation duly formed pursuant to the laws of the State of   ,

and that the foregoing is a true record of a resolution duly adopted at a meeting of the

Board of Directors, and that said meeting was held in accordance with state law and the

Bylaws of the above-named Corporation on   , 19   , and that said

resolution is now in full force and effect without modification or rescission.

IN WITNESS WHEREOF, I have executed my name as Secretary and have hereunto

affixed the corporate seal of the above-named Corporation this   day of   ,

19   .

A True Record.

Attest.

_____
Secretary

RESOLUTION:
PURCHASE REAL ESTATE

WHEREAS, the Corporation requires additional facilities for the operation of its business, and

WHEREAS, it would be desirous to own rather than rent said premises; be it

RESOLVED, that the Corporation purchase and acquire real estate known or described as   from   ,
for the purchase price of $, all as further set forth in a purchase and sales agreement as annexed hereto.

The undersigned hereby certifies that he/she is the duly elected and qualified Secretary and the custodian of the books and records and seal of   ,
a corporation duly formed pursuant to the laws of the State of   ,
and that the foregoing is a true record of a resolution duly adopted at a meeting of the Board of Directors, and that said meeting was held in accordance with state law and the Bylaws of the above-named Corporation on   , 19   , and that said resolution is now in full force and effect without modification or rescission.

IN WITNESS WHEREOF, I have executed my name as Secretary and have hereunto affixed the corporate seal of the above-named Corporation this   day of   ,
19   .

A True Record.

Attest.

_____
Secretary

RESOLUTION:
QUALIFY AS A FOREIGN CORPORATION

WHEREAS, the Corporation has or shall conduct business within the state of

       ; be it

RESOLVED, to have the Corporation qualify as a foreign Corporation in the state of

      .

The undersigned hereby certifies that he/she is the duly elected and qualified Secretary

and the custodian of the books and records and seal of   ,

a corporation duly formed pursuant to the laws of the State of   ,

and that the foregoing is a true record of a resolution duly adopted at a meeting of the

Board of Directors, and that said meeting was held in accordance with state law and the

Bylaws of the above-named Corporation on   , 19   , and that said

resolution is now in full force and effect without modification or rescission.

IN WITNESS WHEREOF, I have executed my name as Secretary and have hereunto

affixed the corporate seal of the above-named Corporation this   day of   ,

19 .

A True Record.

Attest.

_____
Secretary

RESOLUTION:

RATIFY ACTS

WHEREAS,   , as   of the
Corporation, has made a full report to the Board of Directors of all major matters and
actions to which   has been a party; be it

RESOLVED, that the Board does hereby ratify and affirm each and every action
undertaken by   , on behalf of the Corporation
wherein said Board has knowledge of said act and wherein it has been fully and accurately
stated.

The undersigned hereby certifies that he/she is the duly elected and qualified Secretary
and the custodian of the books and records and seal of   ,
a corporation duly formed pursuant to the laws of the State of   ,
and that the foregoing is a true record of a resolution duly adopted at a meeting of the
Board of Directors, and that said meeting was held in accordance with state law and the
Bylaws of the above-named Corporation on   , 19   , and that said
resolution is now in full force and effect without modification or rescission.

IN WITNESS WHEREOF, I have executed my name as Secretary and have hereunto
affixed the corporate seal of the above-named Corporation this   day of   ,
19   .

A True Record.

Attest.

_____
Secretary

RESOLUTION:
RATIFY BOARD OF DIRECTORS ACTIONS

WHEREAS, all actions by the Board of Directors from   , 19   ,

to   , 19   , have been duly presented to the shareholders at a

shareholders meeting duly called and assembled; be it

RESOLVED, that the shareholders of the Corporation do hereby ratify and affirm all

actions of the Board as presented to the shareholders.

The undersigned hereby certifies that he/she is the duly elected and qualified Secretary

and the custodian of the books and records and seal of   ,

a corporation duly formed pursuant to the laws of the State of   ,

and that the foregoing is a true record of a resolution duly adopted at a meeting of the

Stockholders, and that said meeting was held in accordance with state law and the Bylaws

of the above-named Corporation on   , 19   , and that said

resolution is now in full force and effect without modification or rescission.

IN WITNESS WHEREOF, I have executed my name as Secretary and have hereunto

affixed the corporate seal of the above-named Corporation this   day of   ,

19   .

A True Record.

Attest.

_____

Secretary

RESOLUTION:
REACQUIRE AND REDEEM OUTSTANDING SHARES

WHEREAS, the Board of Directors of this Corporation has determined that it is in the best interests of the Corporation to reacquire certain shares of stock from its stockholders, and to thereafter retire said shares as non-voting Treasury stock; be it

RESOLVED, that the Corporation hereby make an offer of redemption to its shareholders in accordance with the terms of offer as are annexed hereto; and

RESOLVED FURTHER, that the President of the Corporation undertake all actions necessary to carry out the foregoing resolution.

The undersigned hereby certifies that he/she is the duly elected and qualified Secretary and the custodian of the books and records and seal of
, a corporation duly formed pursuant to the laws of the State of   ,
and that the foregoing is a true record of a resolution duly adopted at a meeting of the Stockholders, and that said meeting was held in accordance with state law and the Bylaws of the above-named Corporation on   , 19   , and that said resolution is now in full force and effect without modification or rescission.

IN WITNESS WHEREOF, I have executed my name as Secretary and have hereunto affixed the corporate seal of the above-named Corporation this   day of   ,
19   .

A True Record.

Attest.

_____
Secretary

RESOLUTION:
REIMBURSE LENDER

RESOLVED, that the Corporation reimburse   the sum

of $ for monies paid by

in connection with the business of the Corporation, and more particularly:

The undersigned hereby certifies that he/she is the duly elected and qualified Secretary

and the custodian of the books and records and seal of   ,

a corporation duly formed pursuant to the laws of the State of   ,

and that the foregoing is a true record of a resolution duly adopted at a meeting of the

Board of Directors, and that said meeting was held in accordance with state law and the

Bylaws of the above-named Corporation on   , 19   , and that said

resolution is now in full force and effect without modification or rescission.

IN WITNESS WHEREOF, I have executed my name as Secretary and have hereunto

affixed the corporate seal of the above-named Corporation this   day of   ,

19   .

A True Record.

Attest.

_____
Secretary

RESOLUTION:
RETAIN ACCOUNTANT

WHEREAS, the Corporation requires the services of an accountant for general accounting purposes, including the preparation of tax returns; be it

RESOLVED, that the Corporation for its general accounting and tax needs retain the accounting firm of   , upon such terms as may be contained in the proposed terms of engagement annexed hereto or upon such generally prevailing rates as are customarily charged by said accountant.

The undersigned hereby certifies that he/she is the duly elected and qualified Secretary and the custodian of the books and records and seal of   , a corporation duly formed pursuant to the laws of the State of   , and that the foregoing is a true record of a resolution duly adopted at a meeting of the Board of Directors, and that said meeting was held in accordance with state law and the Bylaws of the above-named Corporation on   , 19   , and that said resolution is now in full force and effect without modification or rescission.

IN WITNESS WHEREOF, I have executed my name as Secretary and have hereunto affixed the corporate seal of the above-named Corporation this   day of   , 19   .

A True Record.

Attest.

_____
Secretary

RESOLUTION:
RETAIN ATTORNEY

WHEREAS, the Corporation requires the services of an attorney for its general legal affairs; be it

RESOLVED, that the Corporation, for its general legal needs, appoint the law firm of

as its general counsel; such appointment being further upon those terms as set forth in the proposed terms of engagements annexed hereto or upon such generally prevailing rates as are customarily charged by said attorney.

The undersigned hereby certifies that he/she is the duly elected and qualified Secretary and the custodian of the books and records and seal of   ,

a corporation duly formed pursuant to the laws of the State of   ,

and that the foregoing is a true record of a resolution duly adopted at a meeting of the Board of Directors, and that said meeting was held in accordance with state law and the Bylaws of the above-named Corporation on   , 19   , and that said resolution is now in full force and effect without modification or rescission.

IN WITNESS WHEREOF, I have executed my name as Secretary and have hereunto affixed the corporate seal of the above-named Corporation this   day of   ,

19   .

A True Record.

Attest.

_____
Secretary

RESOLUTION:
RETAIN BUSINESS BROKER

WHEREAS, the Corporation desires to sell its business, and

WHEREAS, the Corporation desires to retain a licensed business broker for said purpose; be it

RESOLVED, that the Corporation retain   as its business broker for purposes of selling the business, said terms of appointment being as contained in a listing agreement annexed hereto.

The undersigned hereby certifies that he/she is the duly elected and qualified Secretary and the custodian of the books and records and seal of   , a corporation duly formed pursuant to the laws of the State of   , and that the foregoing is a true record of a resolution duly adopted at a meeting of the Board of Directors, and that said meeting was held in accordance with state law and the Bylaws of the above-named Corporation on   , 19   , and that said resolution is now in full force and effect without modification or rescission.

IN WITNESS WHEREOF, I have executed my name as Secretary and have hereunto affixed the corporate seal of the above-named Corporation this   day of   , 19   .

A True Record.

Attest.

_____
Secretary

RESOLUTION:
RETAIN CONSULTANT

WHEREAS, the Corporation requires professional assistance in the area of:

; be it

RESOLVED, that the Corporation retain   as

a business consultant for the above general purposes and that the terms of engagement

shall be as contained in the consultant agreement annexed hereto.

The undersigned hereby certifies that he/she is the duly elected and qualified Secretary

and the custodian of the books and records and seal of   ,

a corporation duly formed pursuant to the laws of the State of   ,

and that the foregoing is a true record of a resolution duly adopted at a meeting of the

Board of Directors, and that said meeting was held in accordance with state law and the

Bylaws of the above-named Corporation on   , 19   , and that said

resolution is now in full force and effect without modification or rescission.

IN WITNESS WHEREOF, I have executed my name as Secretary and have hereunto

affixed the corporate seal of the above-named Corporation this   day of   ,

19   .

A True Record.

Attest.

_____
Secretary

RESOLUTION:
RETAIN REAL ESTATE BROKER

WHEREAS, the Corporation is desirous of selling certain real estate, and

WHEREAS, the Corporation desires to retain a licensed real estate broker for that purpose; be it

RESOLVED, that the Corporation retain   as its real estate broker for purposes of selling certain real estate owned by the Corporation known as

          , said terms of appointment as are contained in the broker's agreement annexed hereto.

The undersigned hereby certifies that he/she is the duly elected and qualified Secretary and the custodian of the books and records and seal of   , a corporation duly formed pursuant to the laws of the State of   , and that the foregoing is a true record of a resolution duly adopted at a meeting of the Board of Directors, and that said meeting was held in accordance with state law and the Bylaws of the above-named Corporation on   , 19   , and that said resolution is now in full force and effect without modification or rescission.

IN WITNESS WHEREOF, I have executed my name as Secretary and have hereunto affixed the corporate seal of the above-named Corporation this   day of   , 19   .

A True Record.

Attest.

_____
Secretary

RESOLUTION:
RETAIN SPECIAL ACCOUNTANT

WHEREAS, the Corporation has need of an accountant for the specific purpose of:

; be it

RESOLVED, to appoint   accountant for

said purposes and all matters incidental to said purpose.

Said accountant shall be compensated in accordance with his generally prevailing rates.

The undersigned hereby certifies that he/she is the duly elected and qualified Secretary

and the custodian of the books and records and seal of   ,

a corporation duly formed pursuant to the laws of the State of   ,

and that the foregoing is a true record of a resolution duly adopted at a meeting of the

Board of Directors, and that said meeting was held in accordance with state law and the

Bylaws of the above-named Corporation on   , 19   , and that said

resolution is now in full force and effect without modification or rescission.

IN WITNESS WHEREOF, I have executed my name as Secretary and have hereunto

affixed the corporate seal of the above-named Corporation this   day of   ,

19   .

A True Record.

Attest.

_____
Secretary

RESOLUTION:
RETAIN SPECIAL ATTORNEY

WHEREAS, the Corporation has need for an attorney solely for the specific purpose of:

; be it

RESOLVED, that the Corporation retain   as

special counsel solely for the aforesaid purpose and all matters incidental thereto and that

said counsel shall be compensated in accordance with his generally prevailing rates.

The undersigned hereby certifies that he/she is the duly elected and qualified Secretary

and the custodian of the books and records and seal of   ,

a corporation duly formed pursuant to the laws of the State of   ,

and that the foregoing is a true record of a resolution duly adopted at a meeting of the

Board of Directors, and that said meeting was held in accordance with state law and the

Bylaws of the above-named Corporation on   , 19   , and that said

resolution is now in full force and effect without modification or rescission.

IN WITNESS WHEREOF, I have executed my name as Secretary and have hereunto

affixed the corporate seal of the above-named Corporation this   day of   ,

19   .

A True Record.

Attest.

_____
Secretary

RESOLUTION:
SELL ASSETS SUBJECT TO SHAREHOLDER APPROVAL

WHEREAS, an offer has been made to this Corporation by

to purchase the entire assets of this Corporation for the consideration and upon the terms and conditions set forth in the proposed agreement as annexed, and

WHEREAS, in the opinion of this Board of Directors, it is in the best interests of this Corporation that its entire assets be sold to

upon the price, terms and conditions in the proposed agreement above, be it

RESOLVED, that the offer of said   is hereby accepted, subject to the approval of the stockholders of this Corporation, and

RESOLVED FURTHER, that the President and the Secretary are hereby authorized and directed to make, execute, and deliver the aforementioned agreement upon the adoption of the same by the stockholders of this Corporation, and

RESOLVED FURTHER, that the Secretary of the Corporation notice a special stockholder meeting for the purposes of obtaining stockholder approval to said sale.

The undersigned hereby certifies that he/she is the duly elected and qualified Secretary and the custodian of the books and records and seal of   , a corporation duly formed pursuant to the laws of the State of   , and that the foregoing is a true record of a resolution duly adopted at a meeting of the Board of Directors, and that said meeting was held in accordance with state law and the Bylaws of the above-named Corporation on   , 19   , and that said resolution is now in full force and effect without modification or rescission.

IN WITNESS WHEREOF, I have executed my name as Secretary and have hereunto affixed the corporate seal of the above-named Corporation this   day of   , 19   .

A True Record.

Attest.

_____
Secretary

RESOLUTION:
SELL BUSINESS ASSETS

WHEREAS, the Corporation has received an offer from

to purchase all the assets of the Corporation as a going business concern, all as were particularly set forth in a purchase agreement annexed hereto; and

WHEREAS, in the opinion of the Board, it is in the best interests of the Corporation and its shareholders for the Corporation to sell its assets pursuant to the terms of agreement; be it

RESOLVED, that the offer to purchase the assets of the Corporation is hereby accepted by the Board, but subject to approval and ratification by the requisite number of shareholders of the Corporation; and

RESOLVED FURTHER, that upon shareholder approval, the President of the Corporation undertake all acts and execute all documents as necessary to consummate said transaction upon its terms.

The undersigned hereby certifies that he/she is the duly elected and qualified Secretary and the custodian of the books and records and seal of   ,
a corporation duly formed pursuant to the laws of the State of   ,
and that the foregoing is a true record of a resolution duly adopted at a meeting of the Stockholders, and that said meeting was held in accordance with state law and the Bylaws of the above-named Corporation on   , 19   , and that said resolution is now in full force and effect without modification or rescission.

IN WITNESS WHEREOF, I have executed my name as Secretary and have hereunto affixed the corporate seal of the above-named Corporation this   day of   ,
19   .

A True Record.

Attest.

_____
Secretary

RESOLUTION:
SELL CORPORATE SHARES

WHEREAS,   has duly subscribed for

(   ) shares of the common stock for the aggregate subscription price of

$, and

WHEREAS, the Board of Directors deems it to be in the best interests of the Corporation

to accept said subscription; be it

RESOLVED, that the Corporation does hereby accept the stock subscription of

         , to purchase (   ) shares of the Corporation for $,

and, it is

RESOLVED FURTHER, that upon tender of the subscription price, the Treasurer of the

Corporation issue to   , or his or her nominee, (   ) shares

of the no-par value common stock.

The undersigned hereby certifies that he/she is the duly elected and qualified Secretary

and the custodian of the books and records and seal of   ,

a corporation duly formed pursuant to the laws of the State of   ,

and that the foregoing is a true record of a resolution duly adopted at a meeting of the

Stockholders, and that said meeting was held in accordance with state law and the Bylaws

of the above-named Corporation on   , 19   , and that said

resolution is now in full force and effect without modification or rescission.

IN WITNESS WHEREOF, I have executed my name as Secretary and have hereunto

affixed the corporate seal of the above-named Corporation this   day of   ,

19   .

A True Record.

Attest.

_____

Secretary

RESOLUTION:
SELL EQUIPMENT

WHEREAS, certain equipment owned by the Corporation is no longer necessary for its operation; be it

RESOLVED, to sell certain equipment described as

to   for the sales

price of $.

The undersigned hereby certifies that he/she is the duly elected and qualified Secretary and the custodian of the books and records and seal of   ,

a corporation duly formed pursuant to the laws of the State of   ,

and that the foregoing is a true record of a resolution duly adopted at a meeting of the

Stockholders, and that said meeting was held in accordance with state law and the Bylaws

of the above-named Corporation on   , 19   , and that said

resolution is now in full force and effect without modification or rescission.

IN WITNESS WHEREOF, I have executed my name as Secretary and have hereunto

affixed the corporate seal of the above-named Corporation this   day of   ,

19   .

A True Record.

Attest.

_____
Secretary

RESOLUTION:
SELL MOTOR VEHICLE

WHEREAS, a certain motor vehicle owned by the Corporation is no longer necessary for the proper operation of the business; be it

RESOLVED, to sell a certain motor vehicle described as

to   for the sales

price of $.

The undersigned hereby certifies that he/she is the duly elected and qualified Secretary and the custodian of the books and records and seal of   ,

a corporation duly formed pursuant to the laws of the State of   ,

and that the foregoing is a true record of a resolution duly adopted at a meeting of the Board of Directors, and that said meeting was held in accordance with state law and the Bylaws of the above-named Corporation on   , 19   , and that said resolution is now in full force and effect without modification or rescission.

IN WITNESS WHEREOF, I have executed my name as Secretary and have hereunto affixed the corporate seal of the above-named Corporation this   day of   ,

19   .

A True Record.

Attest.

_____
Secretary

RESOLUTION:
SELL REAL ESTATE

WHEREAS, the Corporation owns certain real estate that is no longer needed for the operation of the business and that it would further be desirous to sell some; be it

RESOLVED, that the Corporation sell real estate known or described as

to

for the purchase price of $, all as set forth in a certain purchase and sales agreement as annexed hereto.

The undersigned hereby certifies that he/she is the duly elected and qualified Secretary and the custodian of the books and records and seal of   ,

a corporation duly formed pursuant to the laws of the State of   ,

and that the foregoing is a true record of a resolution duly adopted at a meeting of the Board of Directors, and that said meeting was held in accordance with state law and the Bylaws of the above-named Corporation on   , 19   , and that said resolution is now in full force and effect without modification or rescission.

IN WITNESS WHEREOF, I have executed my name as Secretary and have hereunto affixed the corporate seal of the above-named Corporation this   day of   ,

19   .

A True Record.

Attest.

_____

Secretary

RESOLUTION:
SETTLE LITIGATION

WHEREAS, the Corporation and   are presently engaged in litigation, and

WHEREAS, an offer of settlement has been proposed, and

WHEREAS, it is in the best interests of the Corporation to accept said settlement and terminate the litigation; be it

RESOLVED, that the Corporation accept the settlement offer as presented to the Board and as set forth in offer of settlement annexed; and, it is

RESOLVED FURTHER, that the President of the Corporation, together with counsel, be authorized to execute and deliver all documents and undertake such acts as are necessary to comply with the terms of settlement.

The undersigned hereby certifies that he/she is the duly elected and qualified Secretary and the custodian of the books and records and seal of   ,
a corporation duly formed pursuant to the laws of the State of   ,
and that the foregoing is a true record of a resolution duly adopted at a meeting of the Board of Directors, and that said meeting was held in accordance with state law and the Bylaws of the above-named Corporation on   , 19   , and that said resolution is now in full force and effect without modification or rescission.

IN WITNESS WHEREOF, I have executed my name as Secretary and have hereunto affixed the corporate seal of the above-named Corporation this   day of   ,
19   .

A True Record.

Attest.

_____
Secretary

RESOLUTION:
SUBLET SPACE

WHEREAS, the Corporation holds certain space that is no longer required for the efficient operation of its business; be it

RESOLVED, that the Corporation sublet certain space at

to   ;

said sublet commencing on   , 19   , and further subject to the terms and conditions of a certain sublet agreement as annexed hereto.

The undersigned hereby certifies that he/she is the duly elected and qualified Secretary and the custodian of the books and records and seal of   ,

a corporation duly formed pursuant to the laws of the State of   ,

and that the foregoing is a true record of a resolution duly adopted at a meeting of the Board of Directors, and that said meeting was held in accordance with state law and the Bylaws of the above-named Corporation on   , 19   , and that said resolution is now in full force and effect without modification or rescission.

IN WITNESS WHEREOF, I have executed my name as Secretary and have hereunto affixed the corporate seal of the above-named Corporation this   day of   ,

19   .

A True Record.

Attest.

_____

Secretary

RESOLUTION:
TERMINATE CONTRACT

WHEREAS, the Corporation and

are presently parties to a contract dated   , 19   , whereby said contract

summarily calls for:

, and

WHEREAS, the Corporation deems it to be in the best interests of both parties to

terminate said contract as to any non-performed part thereon; be it

RESOLVED, that the Corporation herewith terminate said contract on the terms

contained as annexed hereto.

The undersigned hereby certifies that he/she is the duly elected and qualified Secretary

and the custodian of the books and records and seal of   ,

a corporation duly formed pursuant to the laws of the State of   ,

and that the foregoing is a true record of a resolution duly adopted at a meeting of the

Board of Directors, and that said meeting was held in accordance with state law and the

Bylaws of the above-named Corporation on   , 19   , and that said

resolution is now in full force and effect without modification or rescission.

IN WITNESS WHEREOF, I have executed my name as Secretary and have hereunto

affixed the corporate seal of the above-named Corporation this   day of   ,

19   .

A True Record.

Attest.

_____
Secretary

RESOLUTION:
TERMINATE EMPLOYEE

WHEREAS,   in his capacity as   ,

has not fulfilled his responsibilities adequately; be it

RESOLVED, that   's employment with the Corporation

be terminated as of   , 19   , and that

be provided the customary severance pay and benefits.

The undersigned hereby certifies that he/she is the duly elected and qualified Secretary

and the custodian of the books and records and seal of   ,

a corporation duly formed pursuant to the laws of the State of   ,

and that the foregoing is a true record of a resolution duly adopted at a meeting of the

Board of Directors, and that said meeting was held in accordance with state law and the

Bylaws of the above-named Corporation on   , 19   , and that said

resolution is now in full force and effect without modification or rescission.

IN WITNESS WHEREOF, I have executed my name as Secretary and have hereunto

affixed the corporate seal of the above-named Corporation this   day of   ,

19   .

A True Record.

Attest.

_____
Secretary

RESOLUTION:
TERMINATE LEASE

WHEREAS, the Corporation has no further need for certain space that it occupies as a tenant; be it

RESOLVED, to terminate as tenant a certain lease from   ,
as landlord, said lease dated   , 19   , for premises at

The termination date shall be   , 19   , with surrender of the premises by the Corporation on or before said date.

The undersigned hereby certifies that he/she is the duly elected and qualified Secretary and the custodian of the books and records and seal of   ,
a corporation duly formed pursuant to the laws of the State of   ,
and that the foregoing is a true record of a resolution duly adopted at a meeting of the Board of Directors, and that said meeting was held in accordance with state law and the Bylaws of the above-named Corporation on   , 19   , and that said resolution is now in full force and effect without modification or rescission.

IN WITNESS WHEREOF, I have executed my name as Secretary and have hereunto affixed the corporate seal of the above-named Corporation this   day of   , 19   .

A True Record.

Attest.

_____
Secretary

RESOLUTION:
WAIVE RESTRICTIONS ON TRANSFER

RESOLVED, to waive all restrictions of transfer imposed on the shares of stock of the

Corporation for purposes of allowing a transfer of   (   ) shares

of common stock of the Corporation from   to

, provided that said restrictions shall apply to any further

transfer of said shares.

The undersigned hereby certifies that he/she is the duly elected and qualified Secretary

and the custodian of the books and records and seal of   ,

a corporation duly formed pursuant to the laws of the State of   ,

and that the foregoing is a true record of a resolution duly adopted at a meeting of the

Stockholders, and that said meeting was held in accordance with state law and the Bylaws

of the above-named Corporation on   , 19   , and that said

resolution is now in full force and effect without modification or rescission.

IN WITNESS WHEREOF, I have executed my name as Secretary and have hereunto

affixed the corporate seal of the above-named Corporation this   day of   ,

19   .

A True Record.

Attest.

_____
Secretary

Section Six

Dividends

Form D601   Records director's dissent to action taken by the Board of Directors in director's absence.

Form R601   Appoints appraiser to appraise the corporation's assets for the purpose of creating a surplus so a dividend can be paid.

Form R602   Authorizes the corporation to borrow money to pay a dividend.

Form R603   Declares an additional cash dividend to stockholders.

Form R604   Authorizes a cash dividend to be paid to shareholders of record from the corporation's general accounts.

Form R605   Declares an extra dividend to be paid to shareholders of record.

Form R606   Retains the accumulated earnings and declares no dividend to be paid for a specified period to improve the corporation's financial condition.

Form R607   Authorizes corporation to skip a dividend payment during a specified period.

Form R608   States the corporation's dividend policy.

DIRECTOR'S DISSENT TO BOARD ACTION

Mr./Ms.

Secretary

Dear Sir/Madam:

In my capacity as a director of _____, I hereby notify you of my dissent from the action taken by the Board of Directors of _____, at its meeting on _____, 19____, from which I was absent. The action I dissent from was the board's decision to:

I hereby request that you enter my dissent in the minutes of the meeting of _____, 19____, of the Board of Directors, and that you advise each member of the board of this request.

Sincerely,

_____
Director

RESOLUTION:
APPOINT APPRAISER AND APPRAISE ASSETS

WHEREAS, the board has reason to believe that certain assets are carried on the books for an amount not consistent with their true worth; be it

RESOLVED, that the Corporation retain a professional appraiser for purposes of valuing the following described assets of the Corporation:

The undersigned hereby certifies that he/she is the duly elected and qualified Secretary and the custodian of the books and records and seal of

a corporation duly formed pursuant to the laws of the State of

and that the foregoing is a true record of a resolution duly adopted at a meeting of the Board of Directors, and that said meeting was held in accordance with state law and the Bylaws of the above-named Corporation on   , 19   , and that said resolution is now in full force and effect without modification or rescission.

IN WITNESS WHEREOF, I have executed my name as Secretary and have hereunto affixed the corporate seal of the above-named Corporation this   day of   ,
19   .

A True Record.

Attest.

_____
Secretary

RESOLUTION:
APPROVE LOAN TO PAY DIVIDEND

WHEREAS, the Corporation has accumulated a surplus sufficient to pay the declared

dividend of   percent on the common stock payable on   , 19   ,

to stockholders of record at the close of business on   , 19   , and

WHEREAS, the cash surplus can be more advantageously used for the expansion of the

business, be it

RESOLVED, that the President is hereby authorized to transact a loan from

       Bank for the amount of the dividend declared, and

RESOLVED FURTHER, that, upon obtaining the said loan, the Treasurer is hereby

directed and authorized to pay out from the fund so borrowed the declared dividend on

the date specified.

The undersigned hereby certifies that he/she is the duly elected and qualified Secretary

and the custodian of the books and records and seal of   ,

a corporation duly formed pursuant to the laws of the State of   ,

and that the foregoing is a true record of a resolution duly adopted at a meeting of the

Board of Directors, and that said meeting was held in accordance with state law and the

Bylaws of the above-named Corporation on   , 19   , and that said

resolution is now in full force and effect without modification or rescission.

IN WITNESS WHEREOF, I have executed my name as Secretary and have hereunto

affixed the corporate seal of the above-named Corporation this   day of   ,

19   .

A True Record.

Attest.

_____

Secretary

RESOLUTION:
AUTHORIZE ADDITIONAL CASH DIVIDEND

WHEREAS, there are sufficient surplus net earnings of this Corporation to justify the declaration of a larger than customary dividend; be it

RESOLVED, that an additional dividend of   percent is herewith declared upon the common stock of the Corporation, payable on   , 19   , to stockholders of record at the close of business on   , 19   .

The undersigned hereby certifies that he/she is the duly elected and qualified Secretary and the custodian of the books and records and seal of   ,

a corporation duly formed pursuant to the laws of the State of   ,

and that the foregoing is a true record of a resolution duly adopted at a meeting of the Board of Directors, and that said meeting was held in accordance with state law and the Bylaws of the above-named Corporation on   , 19   , and that said resolution is now in full force and effect without modification or rescission.

IN WITNESS WHEREOF, I have executed my name as Secretary and have hereunto affixed the corporate seal of the above-named Corporation this   day of   , 19   .

A True Record.

Attest.

_____
Secretary

RESOLUTION:
AUTHORIZE CASH DIVIDEND

WHEREAS, the Corporation has an accumulated earned surplus of $ as

of   , 19   , and

WHEREAS, the board has determined that a cash dividend can be payable to

shareholders; be it

RESOLVED, that the Corporation issue a quarterly dividend declared payable to

shareholders of record of the common stock, as of   , 19   , in the

amount of $ per share, and

FURTHER RESOLVED, that the treasurer may pay said dividends from the general

accounts of the Corporation.

The undersigned hereby certifies that he/she is the duly elected and qualified Secretary

and the custodian of the books and records and seal of   ,

a corporation duly formed pursuant to the laws of the State of   ,

and that the foregoing is a true record of a resolution duly adopted at a meeting of the

Board of Directors, and that said meeting was held in accordance with state law and the

Bylaws of the above-named Corporation on   , 19   , and that said

resolution is now in full force and effect without modification or rescission.

IN WITNESS WHEREOF, I have executed my name as Secretary and have hereunto

affixed the corporate seal of the above-named Corporation this   day of   ,

19   .

A True Record.

Attest.

_____

RESOLUTION:
DECLARE AN EXTRA DIVIDEND

RESOLVED, that the regular dividend of

dollars ($) per share shall be supplemented by an additional payment of

dollars ($)

per share so that the total amount of the regular dividend and the extra dividend shall be

dollars ($) per share, and

the Treasurer is hereby authorized and directed to set aside a sufficient portion of the

current surplus to satisfy such dividend payment, and the Treasurer is further directed to

make such dividend payable to all shareholders of record at the close of business on the

day of   , 19   .

The undersigned hereby certifies that he/she is the duly elected and qualified Secretary

and the custodian of the books and records and seal of   ,

a corporation duly formed pursuant to the laws of the State of   ,

and that the foregoing is a true record of a resolution duly adopted at a meeting of the

Board of Directors, and that said meeting was held in accordance with state law and the

Bylaws of the above-named Corporation on   , 19   , and that said

resolution is now in full force and effect without modification or rescission.

IN WITNESS WHEREOF, I have executed my name as Secretary and have hereunto

affixed the corporate seal of the above-named Corporation this   day of   ,

19   .

A True Record.

Attest.

_____
Secretary

RESOLUTION:
RETAIN EARNINGS

WHEREAS, the Corporation has an earned surplus from which dividends can be paid, but that preservation of said surplus is necessary to improve the Corporation's financial condition; be it

RESOLVED, that no dividends be declared for the   ending   , 19   , and that the accumulated earnings be added to the surplus account of the Corporation.

The undersigned hereby certifies that he/she is the duly elected and qualified Secretary and the custodian of the books and records and seal of   , a corporation duly formed pursuant to the laws of the State of   , and that the foregoing is a true record of a resolution duly adopted at a meeting of the Board of Directors, and that said meeting was held in accordance with state law and the Bylaws of the above-named Corporation on   , 19   , and that said resolution is now in full force and effect without modification or rescission.

IN WITNESS WHEREOF, I have executed my name as Secretary and have hereunto affixed the corporate seal of the above-named Corporation this   day of   , 19   .

A True Record.

Attest.

_____
Secretary

RESOLUTION:
SKIP A DIVIDEND

RESOLVED, that a regular dividend will not be declared on the common stock of this Corporation for the   quarter of 19   , and that the amount so saved is to be retained by the Corporation in its surplus account.

The undersigned hereby certifies that he/she is the duly elected and qualified Secretary and the custodian of the books and records and seal of   ,

a corporation duly formed pursuant to the laws of the State of   ,

and that the foregoing is a true record of a resolution duly adopted at a meeting of the Board of Directors, and that said meeting was held in accordance with state law and the Bylaws of the above-named Corporation on   , 19   , and that said resolution is now in full force and effect without modification or rescission.

IN WITNESS WHEREOF, I have executed my name as Secretary and have hereunto affixed the corporate seal of the above-named Corporation this   day of   ,

19   .

A True Record.

Attest.

_____

Secretary

RESOLUTION:
STATE CORPORATION'S DIVIDEND POLICY

RESOLVED, that it is this Corporation's dividend policy to pay a dividend of

dollars ($) per

annum on the common stock of the Corporation, payable in quarterly installments on the

first day of   ,   ,

and   , if (1) the earnings of the

Corporation support such payments under the laws of the State of   ,

and (2) it is determined that the payment of such dividends is in the best interests of the

Corporation.

The undersigned hereby certifies that he/she is the duly elected and qualified Secretary

and the custodian of the books and records and seal of   ,

a corporation duly formed pursuant to the laws of the state of

and that the foregoing is a true record of a resolution duly adopted at a meeting of the

Board of Directors, and that said meeting was held in accordance with state law and the

Bylaws of the above-named Corporation on   , 19   , and that said

resolution is now in full force and effect without modification or rescission.

IN WITNESS WHEREOF, I have executed my name as Secretary and have hereunto

affixed the corporate seal of the above-named Corporation this   day of   ,

19   .

A True Record.

Attest.

_____

Secretary

Section Seven

Compensation and Benefits

Form R701	Adopts a severance benefit plan for certain key employees of the corporation.
Form R702	Adopts a cafeteria plan of benefits for the corporation's employees.
Form R703	Adopts an employee benefit plan to improve morale and aid in recruitment and retention of employees.
Form R704	Adopts an employee welfare plan to provide for the general welfare of the corporation's employees.
Form R705	Adopts a wage continuation plan for sick and injured employees.
Form R706	Approves a 401K retirement plan for the corporation's employees.
Form R707	Approves a simplified employee pension plan administered by the corporation on behalf of its employees.
Form R708	Approves a cash bonus for a specific employee.
Form R709	Approves an employee loan program.
Form R710	Approves an employee scholarship program for eligible children of employees of the corporation.
Form R711	Approves financial counseling benefits for employees.
Form R712	Approves group legal benefits for employees.
Form R713	Approves a special honorarium to recognize services of a specific employee.
Form R714	Approves life insurance benefits for employees.

Form R715   Approves officer bonuses.

Form R716   Approves a pension plan for employees.

Form R717   Approves a profit-sharing plan for employees.

Form R718   Approves a qualified stock option plan for employees of the corporation.

Form R719   Approves a split-dollar insurance benefit program for employees of the corporation.

Form R720   Approves a stock bonus to directors of the corporation.

Form R721   Approves a stock option plan for sale and issuance to the executives and key employees of the corporation.

Form R722   Authorizes a bonus to an officer of the corporation.

Form R723   Authorizes an officer of the corporation to establish a credit account with a specific party to pay business-related expenses.

Form R724   Authorizes Christmas bonuses for employees of the corporation.

Form R725   Authorizes the corporation to apply for membership at a specific Country Club for business purposes.

Form R726   Authorizes compensation to be paid to directors upon their attendance at meetings.

Form R727   Authorizes group medical and dental benefits for employees of the corporation.

Form R728   Authorizes a leave of absence for a specific employee.

Form R729   Authorizes a raise for an officer of the corporation.

Form R730   Establishes the salary of a position with the corporation.

Form R731   Authorizes a charitable contribution to be made on behalf of the corporation.

Form R732   Modifies the salaries of corporate officers.

Form R733   Authorizes payment of bonuses to corporate officers.

Form R734   Requires each officer to repay excess salary or compensation that has been disallowed by the IRS.

Form R735   Authorizes stock bonus for the officers of the corporation.

Form R736   Terminates the salaries of corporate officers.

RESOLUTION:
ADOPT A SEVERANCE BENEFIT PLAN

WHEREAS, the Board of Directors of this Corporation deems it to be in the best interests of the Corporation and certain key employees to increase their pension contribution limit by establishing a Severance Benefit Plan under Section 419 (A) of the Internal Revenue Code; be it

RESOLVED, that the Corporation adopt a Severance Benefit Plan under Section 419 (A), all as set forth on the proposed plan as annexed; and, be it

RESOLVED FURTHER, that the President and/or Treasurer of the Corporation undertake all actions deemed necessary to implement and administer said plan.

The undersigned hereby certifies that he/she is the duly elected and qualified Secretary and the custodian of the books and records and seal of   ,
a corporation duly formed pursuant to the laws of the State of   ,
and that the foregoing is a true record of a resolution duly adopted at a meeting of the Board of Directors, and that said meeting was held in accordance with state law and the Bylaws of the above-named Corporation on   , 19   , and that said resolution is now in full force and effect without modification or rescission.

IN WITNESS WHEREOF, I have executed my name as Secretary and have hereunto affixed the corporate seal of the above-named Corporation this   day of   ,
19   .

A True Record.

Attest.

_____
Secretary

RESOLUTION:
ADOPT CAFETERIA PLAN OF BENEFITS

WHEREAS, the Board of Directors has determined that it would be in the best interests of the Corporation and its employees to adopt a "Cafeteria Plan" of fringe benefits, so-called; be it

RESOLVED, that the Corporation adopt a so-called "Cafeteria Plan" of benefits to its employees, all in accordance with the specifications annexed hereto; and, be it

RESOLVED FURTHER, that the President and/or Treasurer of the Corporation undertake all actions necessary to implement and administer said plan.

The undersigned hereby certifies that he/she is the duly elected and qualified Secretary and the custodian of the books and records and seal of   ,
a corporation duly formed pursuant to the laws of the State of   ,
and that the foregoing is a true record of a resolution duly adopted at a meeting of the Board of Directors, and that said meeting was held in accordance with state law and the Bylaws of the above-named Corporation on   , 19   , and that said resolution is now in full force and effect without modification or rescission.

IN WITNESS WHEREOF, I have executed my name as Secretary and have hereunto affixed the corporate seal of the above-named Corporation this   day of   ,
19   .

A True Record.

Attest.

_____
Secretary

RESOLUTION:
ADOPT EMPLOYEE BENEFIT PLAN

WHEREAS, it shall improve employee morale and aid in the recruitment of new employees and retention of existing employees if the Corporation establish an Employee Benefit Plan (Plan), and

WHEREAS, the Board of Directors has considered the Plan as annexed and believes it to be in the best interests of the Corporation to adopt; be it

RESOLVED, that the Board of Directors approves the adoption of the Plan as annexed hereto, and subject to further approval and ratification of same by the shareholders with requisite voting powers, and be it

RESOLVED FURTHER, that upon shareholder approval, the officers of the Corporation undertake all actions necessary to implement the Plan.

The undersigned hereby certifies that he/she is the duly elected and qualified Secretary and the custodian of the books and records and seal of   ,

a corporation duly formed pursuant to the laws of the State of   ,

and that the foregoing is a true record of a resolution duly adopted at a meeting of the Board of Directors, and that said meeting was held in accordance with state law and the Bylaws of the above-named Corporation on   , 19   , and that said resolution is now in full force and effect without modification or rescission.

IN WITNESS WHEREOF, I have executed my name as Secretary and have hereunto affixed the corporate seal of the above-named Corporation this   day of   ,

19   .

A True Record.

Attest.

_____

Secretary

RESOLUTION:
ADOPT EMPLOYEE WELFARE PLAN

WHEREAS, the Board of Directors of this Corporation has deemed it advisable to adopt an Employee Welfare Plan to provide for the general welfare of its employees; be it

RESOLVED, that this Corporation adopt an Employee Welfare Plan in accordance with the provisions and specifications as have been presented to and reviewed by this Board, a copy of which is annexed hereto; and, be it

RESOLVED FURTHER, that the President and/or Treasurer of this Corporation undertake such action as is necessary to implement and administer said plan.

The undersigned hereby certifies that he/she is the duly elected and qualified Secretary and the custodian of the books and records and seal of   ,
a corporation duly formed pursuant to the laws of the State of   ,
and that the foregoing is a true record of a resolution duly adopted at a meeting of the Board of Directors, and that said meeting was held in accordance with state law and the Bylaws of the above-named Corporation on   , 19   , and that said resolution is now in full force and effect without modification or rescission.

IN WITNESS WHEREOF, I have executed my name as Secretary and have hereunto affixed the corporate seal of the above-named Corporation this   day of   ,
19   .

A True Record.

Attest.

_____

Secretary

RESOLUTION:
ADOPT WAGE CONTINUATION PLAN

WHEREAS, the officers of this Corporation, after careful deliberation, considered a plan providing for wage payments to sick and injured employees, and

WHEREAS, the officers have presented to this meeting their recommendation for the adoption of a Wage Continuation Plan, a copy of which is attached to and made a part of this Resolution, be it

RESOLVED, that the Board of Directors hereby adopts the attached Wage Continuation Plan, and that the Treasurer of this Corporation is hereby authorized and directed to make payments to eligible employees in accordance with said Plan.

The undersigned hereby certifies that he/she is the duly elected and qualified Secretary and the custodian of the books and records and seal of

a corporation duly formed pursuant to the laws of the State of

and that the foregoing is a true record of a resolution duly adopted at a meeting of the Board of Directors, and that said meeting was held in accordance with state law and the Bylaws of the above-named Corporation on   , 19   , and that said resolution is now in full force and effect without modification or rescission.

IN WITNESS WHEREOF, I have executed my name as Secretary and have hereunto affixed the corporate seal of the above-named Corporation this   day of   ,
19   .

A True Record.

Attest.

_____
Secretary

RESOLUTION:
APPROVE A 401K RETIREMENT PLAN

WHEREAS, the Board of Directors of the Corporation deems it to be in the best interests of the Corporation and its employees to establish a so-called 401 (K) qualified cash and deferred retirement arrangement (CODA) for its employees; be it

RESOLVED, that the Corporation adopt the proposed 401 (K) plan as is annexed hereto, conditional, however, upon counsel for the Corporation obtaining from the IRS a favorable ruling that said plan qualifies as a qualified-defined benefit plan; and

RESOLVED FURTHER, that upon satisfaction of the foregoing condition, the President and/or Treasurer of the Corporation undertake all actions necessary to implement and administer said plan.

The undersigned hereby certifies that he/she is the duly elected and qualified Secretary and the custodian of the books and records and seal of   ,
a corporation duly formed pursuant to the laws of the State of   ,
and that the foregoing is a true record of a resolution duly adopted at a meeting of the Board of Directors, and that said meeting was held in accordance with state law and the Bylaws of the above-named Corporation on   , 19   , and that said resolution is now in full force and effect without modification or rescission.

IN WITNESS WHEREOF, I have executed my name as Secretary and have hereunto affixed the corporate seal of the above-named Corporation this   day of   ,
19   .

A True Record.

Attest.

_____
Secretary

RESOLUTION:
APPROVE A SIMPLIFIED EMPLOYEE PENSION PLAN

WHEREAS, the Board of Directors deems it advisable to establish a Simplified Employee Pension Plan (SEP) on behalf of its employees, whereby the Corporation shall make contributions to the IRA accounts of its employees; be it

RESOLVED, that the Corporation establish and administer for its employees a Simplified Employee Pension Plan (SEP, so-called) pursuant to Internal Revenue regulations and as further specified on the proposed plan, annexed, and be it

RESOLVED FURTHER, that the President and/or Treasurer undertake all actions necessary to implement and administer said plan.

The undersigned hereby certifies that he/she is the duly elected and qualified Secretary and the custodian of the books and records and seal of _____ , a corporation duly formed pursuant to the laws of the State of _____ , and that the foregoing is a true record of a resolution duly adopted at a meeting of the Board of Directors, and that said meeting was held in accordance with state law and the Bylaws of the above-named Corporation on _____ , 19 ____ , and that said resolution is now in full force and effect without modification or rescission.

IN WITNESS WHEREOF, I have executed my name as Secretary and have hereunto affixed the corporate seal of the above-named Corporation this ____ day of _____ , 19 ____ .

A True Record.

Attest.

_____
Secretary

RESOLUTION:
APPROVE CASH BONUS

WHEREAS, in recognition of the fact that

has performed meritoriously on behalf of the Corporation and has through diligent effort

materially improved the profits of the Corporation, be it

RESOLVED, that said   be paid a cash bonus of

$ in addition to the regular compensation, and that said bonus be paid

as soon as practicable in the discretion of the Treasurer.

The undersigned hereby certifies that he/she is the duly elected and qualified Secretary

and the custodian of the books and records and seal of   ,

a corporation duly formed pursuant to the laws of the State of   ,

and that the foregoing is a true record of a resolution duly adopted at a meeting of the

Board of Directors, and that said meeting was held in accordance with state law and the

Bylaws of the above-named Corporation on   , 19   , and that said

resolution is now in full force and effect without modification or rescission.

IN WITNESS WHEREOF, I have executed my name as Secretary and have hereunto

affixed the corporate seal of the above-named Corporation this   day of   ,

19   .

A True Record.

Attest.

_____
Secretary

RESOLUTION:
APPROVE EMPLOYEE LOAN PROGRAM

WHEREAS, the Board of Directors deems it advisable to institute a loan program for purposes of advancing loans to employees of the Corporation who will use said loan proceeds for purposes of advancing their own education or the education of their children; and

WHEREAS, the Board wishes to adopt a specific policy for said loan program benefit; be it

RESOLVED, that the Corporation adopt an Educational Loan Plan in accordance with the specification for said program as presented to the Board and annexed hereto, and, it is

RESOLVED FURTHER, that the President and/or Treasurer of the Corporation take all action necessary to implement and administer said plan.

The undersigned hereby certifies that he/she is the duly elected and qualified Secretary and the custodian of the books and records and seal of   ,

a corporation duly formed pursuant to the laws of the State of   ,

and that the foregoing is a true record of a resolution duly adopted at a meeting of the Board of Directors, and that said meeting was held in accordance with state law and the Bylaws of the above-named Corporation on   , 19   , and that said resolution is now in full force and effect without modification or rescission.

IN WITNESS WHEREOF, I have executed my name as Secretary and have hereunto affixed the corporate seal of the above-named Corporation this   day of   ,

19   .

A True Record.

Attest.

_____
Secretary

RESOLUTION:
APPROVE EMPLOYEE SCHOLARSHIP BENEFITS

WHEREAS, this Board of Directors deems it advisable for the Corporation to institute a program whereby eligible children of employees of the Corporation can obtain from the Corporation award scholarships to be used in the furtherance of their education; be it

RESOLVED, the Board adopts a certain Scholarship Aid Program in accordance with the specifications of said program as presented to the Board and annexed hereto; and, be it

RESOLVED FURTHER, that the President and/or Treasurer of the Corporation undertake all actions necessary to implement and administer said program.

The undersigned hereby certifies that he/she is the duly elected and qualified Secretary and the custodian of the books and records and seal of   ,
a corporation duly formed pursuant to the laws of the State of   ,
and that the foregoing is a true record of a resolution duly adopted at a meeting of the Board of Directors, and that said meeting was held in accordance with state law and the Bylaws of the above-named Corporation on   , 19   , and that said resolution is now in full force and effect without modification or rescission.

IN WITNESS WHEREOF, I have executed my name as Secretary and have hereunto affixed the corporate seal of the above-named Corporation this   day of   ,
19   .

A True Record.

Attest.

_____
Secretary

RESOLUTION:
APPROVE FINANCIAL COUNSELING BENEFITS

WHEREAS, the Board of Directors of this Corporation deems it advisable to provide employees professional financial counseling at a cost to be entirely borne by the Corporation; be it

RESOLVED, that the Corporation adopt a Financial Counseling Plan for its employees on those specifications as have been presented to this Board and are annexed hereto; and

RESOLVED FURTHER, that the President and/or Treasurer of this Corporation is directed to undertake all actions as are necessary to implement and administer said plan.

The undersigned hereby certifies that he/she is the duly elected and qualified Secretary and the custodian of the books and records and seal of   ,

a corporation duly formed pursuant to the laws of the State of   ,

and that the foregoing is a true record of a resolution duly adopted at a meeting of the Board of Directors, and that said meeting was held in accordance with state law and the Bylaws of the above-named Corporation on   , 19   , and that said resolution is now in full force and effect without modification or rescission.

IN WITNESS WHEREOF, I have executed my name as Secretary and have hereunto affixed the corporate seal of the above-named Corporation this   day of   , 19   .

A True Record.

Attest.

_____
Secretary

RESOLUTION:
APPROVE GROUP LEGAL BENEFITS

WHEREAS, the Board of Directors of this Corporation deems it advisable to institute a group legal services plan for purposes of providing low-cost or no-cost legal services to employees and members of their families; be it

RESOLVED, that the Corporation adopt a Group Legal Services Plan in accordance with the specifications for a Group Legal Services Plan as presented to this Board and annexed hereto; and

RESOLVED FURTHER, that the President and/or Treasurer of the Corporation undertake all actions as are necessary to implement and administer said program.

The undersigned hereby certifies that he/she is the duly elected and qualified Secretary and the custodian of the books and records and seal of   ,

a corporation duly formed pursuant to the laws of the State of   ,

and that the foregoing is a true record of a resolution duly adopted at a meeting of the Board of Directors, and that said meeting was held in accordance with state law and the Bylaws of the above-named Corporation on   , 19   , and that said resolution is now in full force and effect without modification or rescission.

IN WITNESS WHEREOF, I have executed my name as Secretary and have hereunto affixed the corporate seal of the above-named Corporation this   day of   ,
19   .

A True Record.

Attest.

_____
Secretary

RESOLUTION:
APPROVE HONORARIUM

WHEREAS, valuable services have been rendered to this Corporation by

, and

WHEREAS, the Board wishes to recognize said services and reward same by payment of a special honorarium; be it

RESOLVED, that the Corporation pay an honorarium of $ to

, in recognition of the special services granted the Corporation, and that the directors of the Corporation be directed to pay same forthwith.

The undersigned hereby certifies that he/she is the duly elected and qualified Secretary and the custodian of the books and records and seal of   ,
a corporation duly formed pursuant to the laws of the State of   ,
and that the foregoing is a true record of a resolution duly adopted at a meeting of the Board of Directors, and that said meeting was held in accordance with state law and the Bylaws of the above-named Corporation on   , 19   , and that said resolution is now in full force and effect without modification or rescission.

IN WITNESS WHEREOF, I have executed my name as Secretary and have hereunto affixed the corporate seal of the above-named Corporation this   day of   ,
19   .

A True Record.

Attest.

_____
Secretary

RESOLUTION:
APPROVE LIFE INSURANCE BENEFITS

WHEREAS, it is the decision of the Board of Directors that the availability of a group life program is in the best interests of the Corporation as it will encourage improved employee relations and aid in the recruitment and retention of valuable employees and serve generally as a benefit to employees, be it

RESOLVED, that the Corporation purchase and acquire group insurance for those employees entitled to participate in said benefit in that said employee has been employed by the Corporation for at least   years, that the amount of insurance coverage be $ per employee, and that the entire cost of said insurance be borne by the Corporation. It is

RESOLVED FURTHER, that the President of the Corporation obtain said insurance from such insurance firm or firms which in the President's judgment is most satisfactory.

The undersigned hereby certifies that he/she is the duly elected and qualified Secretary and the custodian of the books and records and seal of   ,
a corporation duly formed pursuant to the laws of the State of   ,
and that the foregoing is a true record of a resolution duly adopted at a meeting of the Board of Directors, and that said meeting was held in accordance with state law and the Bylaws of the above-named Corporation on   , 19   , and that said resolution is now in full force and effect without modification or rescission.

IN WITNESS WHEREOF, I have executed my name as Secretary and have hereunto affixed the corporate seal of the above-named Corporation this   day of   ,
19   .

A True Record.

Attest.

_____
Secretary

RESOLUTION:
APPROVE OFFICER BONUSES

WHEREAS, the Board is desirous of making certain cash bonuses to the various officers of the Corporation, all in recognition of their devoted service to the Corporation over this year; be it

RESOLVED, that the officers of the Corporation receive the bonuses as follows:

To_____ Chairman, $_____

To_____ President, $_____

To_____ Vice President, $_____

To_____ Treasurer, $_____

To_____ Secretary, $_____

RESOLVED FURTHER, that the Treasurer of the Corporation is directed to issue the above cash bonuses in accordance with the above specifications.

The undersigned hereby certifies that he/she is the duly elected and qualified Secretary and the custodian of the books and records and seal of

a corporation duly formed pursuant to the laws of the State of

and that the foregoing is a true record of a resolution duly adopted at a meeting of the Board of Directors, and that said meeting was held in accordance with state law and the Bylaws of the above-named Corporation on   , 19   , and that said resolution is now in full force and effect without modification or rescission.

IN WITNESS WHEREOF, I have executed my name as Secretary and have hereunto affixed the corporate seal of the above-named Corporation this   day of   ,
19   .

A True Record.

Attest.

_____
Secretary

RESOLUTION:
APPROVE PENSION PLAN

WHEREAS, the Board of Directors of this Corporation deems it advisable to provide for the financial and retirement security of its employees; be it

RESOLVED, that the Corporation adopt a Pension Plan in accordance with the provisions and specifications as have been presented to and reviewed by this Board, and as said specifications are further annexed hereto; and, be it

RESOLVED FURTHER, that the President and/or Treasurer of the Corporation be directed to undertake such acts as are necessary to implement and administer said plan.

The undersigned hereby certifies that he/she is the duly elected and qualified Secretary and the custodian of the books and records and seal of   ,
a corporation duly formed pursuant to the laws of the State of   ,
and that the foregoing is a true record of a resolution duly adopted at a meeting of the Board of Directors, and that said meeting was held in accordance with state law and the Bylaws of the above-named Corporation on   , 19 , and that said resolution is now in full force and effect without modification or rescission.

IN WITNESS WHEREOF, I have executed my name as Secretary and have hereunto affixed the corporate seal of the above-named Corporation this   day of   ,
19 .

A True Record.

Attest.

_____
Secretary

RESOLUTION:
APPROVE PROFIT-SHARING PLAN

WHEREAS, the Board of Directors of this Corporation considers it to be in the best interests of the Corporation to adopt an employee Profit-Sharing Plan as a means of improving employee incentive and performance; be it

RESOLVED, that the Corporation adopt an employee Profit-Sharing Plan as presented to the Board, the specifications of which are annexed hereto, provided however that adoption shall be conditional upon (1) duly voted shareholder approval, and (2) a favorable ruling from the IRS that the plan, as constituted, qualifies under Sections 401 (a) and 404 of the Internal Revenue Code of 1954, as amended, and

RESOLVED FURTHER, that upon satisfaction of the conditions stated, the President and/or Treasurer undertake all actions as are necessary to implement and administer the plan.

The undersigned hereby certifies that he/she is the duly elected and qualified Secretary and the custodian of the books and records and seal of

a corporation duly formed pursuant to the laws of the State of

and that the foregoing is a true record of a resolution duly adopted at a meeting of the Board of Directors, and that said meeting was held in accordance with state law and the Bylaws of the above-named Corporation on   , 19   , and that said resolution is now in full force and effect without modification or rescission.

IN WITNESS WHEREOF, I have executed my name as Secretary and have hereunto affixed the corporate seal of the above-named Corporation this   day of   , 19   .

A True Record.

Attest.

_____
Secretary

RESOLUTION:
APPROVE QUALIFIED STOCK OPTION PLAN

WHEREAS, the Board of Directors of this Corporation has determined that certain officers and key employees should have available to them an option to buy shares of the Corporation under a qualified Stock Option Plan; be it

RESOLVED, that the Corporation adopt a Stock Option Plan in accordance with the provisions and specifications of the Stock Option Plan presented to and reviewed by the Board, a copy of said specifications being annexed hereto; and, be it

RESOLVED FURTHER, that the Corporation shall set aside a total of

(   ) shares of the common stock of the Corporation for sale to officers and key employees under the plan, and all as further approved by the shareholders; and, be it

RESOLVED FURTHER, that the President and/or Treasurer of the Corporation shall undertake all actions necessary to implement and administer said plan.

The undersigned hereby certifies that he/she is the duly elected and qualified Secretary and the custodian of the books and records and seal of   ,

a corporation duly formed pursuant to the laws of the State of   ,

and that the foregoing is a true record of a resolution duly adopted at a meeting of the Board of Directors, and that said meeting was held in accordance with state law and the Bylaws of the above-named Corporation on   , 19   , and that said resolution is now in full force and effect without modification or rescission.

IN WITNESS WHEREOF, I have executed my name as Secretary and have hereunto affixed the corporate seal of the above-named Corporation this   day of   ,

19   .

A True Record.

Attest.

_____
Secretary

RESOLUTION:
APPROVE SPLIT-DOLLAR INSURANCE

WHEREAS, it is the decision of the Board of Directors that a Split-Dollar Insurance Program be instituted as a fringe benefit and to make available adequate insurance to protect their families in the event of death; be it

RESOLVED, that the Corporation negotiate the purchase of Split-Dollar Life Insurance and adopt a Split-Dollar Insurance Benefit Program, all in accordance with the specifications for said insurance program as presented to the Board and annexed hereto. And, it is

RESOLVED FURTHER, that the President of the Corporation be authorized to negotiate and purchase such insurance from such underwriters, and on such terms as the president deems to be in the best interests of the Corporation.

The undersigned hereby certifies that he/she is the duly elected and qualified Secretary and the custodian of the books and records and seal of   ,

a corporation duly formed pursuant to the laws of the State of   ,

and that the foregoing is a true record of a resolution duly adopted at a meeting of the Board of Directors, and that said meeting was held in accordance with state law and the Bylaws of the above-named Corporation on   , 19   , and that said resolution is now in full force and effect without modification or rescission.

IN WITNESS WHEREOF, I have executed my name as Secretary and have hereunto affixed the corporate seal of the above-named Corporation this   day of   ,

19   .

A True Record.

Attest.

_____

Secretary

RESOLUTION:
APPROVE STOCK BONUS TO DIRECTORS

WHEREAS, the Board of Directors is desirous of making certain bonuses available to the officers of the Corporation in the form of shares of common stock; be it

RESOLVED, that the following officers of the Corporation be issued as a bonus the number of shares of common stock of the Corporation as is set forth opposite their respective names:

Name	Title	Number of Shares
_____	_____	_____
_____	_____	_____
_____	_____	_____
_____	_____	_____

The undersigned hereby certifies that he/she is the duly elected and qualified Secretary and the custodian of the books and records and seal of _____ ,

a corporation duly formed pursuant to the laws of the State of _____ ,

and that the foregoing is a true record of a resolution duly adopted at a meeting of the Board of Directors, and that said meeting was held in accordance with state law and the Bylaws of the above-named Corporation on _____ , 19____ , and that said resolution is now in full force and effect without modification or rescission.

IN WITNESS WHEREOF, I have executed my name as Secretary and have hereunto affixed the corporate seal of the above-named Corporation this ____ day of _____ ,

19____ .

A True Record.

Attest.

_____
Secretary

RESOLUTION:
APPROVE STOCK OPTION PLAN

RESOLVED, that the Stock Option Plan attached to this resolution is hereby approved, and

RESOLVED FURTHER, that the Board of Directors is hereby authorized to set aside a total of   (   ) shares of the common stock without par value of this Corporation, pursuant to the increase in the capital stock duly authorized by the stockholders of this Corporation on   , 19   , for sale and issuance to the executives and key employees of this Corporation upon the terms of said Stock Option Plan.

The undersigned hereby certifies that he/she is the duly elected and qualified Secretary and the custodian of the books and records and seal of   , a corporation duly formed pursuant to the laws of the State of   , and that the foregoing is a true record of a resolution duly adopted at a meeting of the Board of Directors, and that said meeting was held in accordance with state law and the Bylaws of the above-named Corporation on   , 19   , and that said resolution is now in full force and effect without modification or rescission.

IN WITNESS WHEREOF, I have executed my name as Secretary and have hereunto affixed the corporate seal of the above-named Corporation this   day of   , 19   .

A True Record.

Attest.

_____

RESOLUTION:
AUTHORIZE BONUS BASED ON PROFITS

RESOLVED, that there shall be paid as special compensation for the services rendered

by   as   of this

Corporation, at   percent (%) of the net profits of this Corporation

during the year 19   , as evidenced by the books of the Corporation, but shall not exceed

the sum of

Dollars ($), the said special compensation to be paid to

at the end of the fiscal year 19   , and

RESOLVED FURTHER, that for the purpose of fixing such compensation, net profits

shall mean the amount available on net income after deductions for interest on

indebtedness, expenses, all accrued taxes, and preferred dividends.

The undersigned hereby certifies that he/she is the duly elected and qualified Secretary

and the custodian of the books and records and seal of   ,

a corporation duly formed pursuant to the laws of the State of   ,

and that the foregoing is a true record of a resolution duly adopted at a meeting of the

Board of Directors, and that said meeting was held in accordance with state law and the

Bylaws of the above-named Corporation on   , 19   , and that said

resolution is now in full force and effect without modification or rescission.

IN WITNESS WHEREOF, I have executed my name as Secretary and have hereunto

affixed the corporate seal of the above-named Corporation this   day of   ,

19   .

A True Record.

Attest.

_____

Secretary

RESOLUTION:
AUTHORIZE CHARGE ACCOUNT

RESOLVED, that   as   of
the Corporation is hereby authorized to establish a credit account with
                              , and to charge to said account any travel, entertainment and
other expenses related to the ordinary and necessary trade or business of this Corporation,
which expenses the Treasurer is hereby authorized and directed to pay as they become
due.

The undersigned hereby certifies that he/she is the duly elected and qualified Secretary
and the custodian of the books and records and seal of   ,
a corporation duly formed pursuant to the laws of the State of   ,
and that the foregoing is a true record of a resolution duly adopted at a meeting of the
Board of Directors, and that said meeting was held in accordance with state law and the
Bylaws of the above-named Corporation on   , 19   , and that said
resolution is now in full force and effect without modification or rescission.

IN WITNESS WHEREOF, I have executed my name as Secretary and have hereunto
affixed the corporate seal of the above-named Corporation this   day of   ,
19   .

A True Record.

Attest.

_____
                                                        Secretary

RESOLUTION:
AUTHORIZE CHRISTMAS BONUSES

WHEREAS, it is in the best interests of the Corporation to motivate its employees with a Christmas bonus; be it

RESOLVED, that the Corporation allocate the sum of

Dollars ($) for Christmas bonuses, and

FURTHER RESOLVED, that bonuses be paid to each employee in accordance with the Christmas Bonus Schedule as annexed hereto.

The undersigned hereby certifies that he/she is the duly elected and qualified Secretary and the custodian of the books and records and seal of   ,

a corporation duly formed pursuant to the laws of the State of   ,

and that the foregoing is a true record of a resolution duly adopted at a meeting of the Board of Directors, and that said meeting was held in accordance with state law and the Bylaws of the above-named Corporation on   , 19   , and that said resolution is now in full force and effect without modification or rescission.

IN WITNESS WHEREOF, I have executed my name as Secretary and have hereunto affixed the corporate seal of the above-named Corporation this   day of   ,

19   .

A True Record.

Attest.

_____

Secretary

RESOLUTION:
AUTHORIZE COUNTRY CLUB MEMBERSHIP

WHEREAS, the Board of Directors has determined that a Country Club membership would enhance the ability of the Corporation to entertain business clients and thereupon conduct more business; be it

RESOLVED, that the Corporation apply for membership at the _____ Country Club, either in its own name or in the name of _____ as _____ of the Corporation; and that the Corporation pay all costs associated with membership or related to the entertainment of business clients.

The undersigned hereby certifies that he/she is the duly elected and qualified Secretary and the custodian of the books and records and seal of _____ , a corporation duly formed pursuant to the laws of the State of _____ , and that the foregoing is a true record of a resolution duly adopted at a meeting of the Board of Directors, and that said meeting was held in accordance with state law and the Bylaws of the above-named Corporation on _____ , 19 ___ , and that said resolution is now in full force and effect without modification or rescission.

IN WITNESS WHEREOF, I have executed my name as Secretary and have hereunto affixed the corporate seal of the above-named Corporation this ___ day of _____ , 19 ___ .

A True Record.

Attest.

_____
Secretary

RESOLUTION:
AUTHORIZE DIRECTORS' COMPENSATION

WHEREAS, it is in the best interests of the Corporation to provide compensation to directors upon their attendance at meetings; be it

RESOLVED, that the Corporation pay to each director attending any regular or special meeting of the board the sum of $ per meeting, inclusive of any adjournment thereof, and that said compensation policy commence with the next held meeting of the board.

The undersigned hereby certifies that he/she is the duly elected and qualified Secretary and the custodian of the books and records and seal of   ,
a corporation duly formed pursuant to the laws of the State of   ,
and that the foregoing is a true record of a resolution duly adopted at a meeting of the Board of Directors, and that said meeting was held in accordance with state law and the Bylaws of the above-named Corporation on   , 19   , and that said resolution is now in full force and effect without modification or rescission.

IN WITNESS WHEREOF, I have executed my name as Secretary and have hereunto affixed the corporate seal of the above-named Corporation this   day of   ,
19   .

A True Record.

Attest.

_____
Secretary

RESOLUTION:
AUTHORIZE GROUP MEDICAL/DENTAL BENEFITS

WHEREAS, the Board of Directors has determined that it is in the best interests of the Corporation to offer its employees a Group Medical/Dental Plan; be it

RESOLVED, that the Corporation adopt the Group Medical/Dental Plan as presented to and reviewed by the board and is further annexed hereto, and

RESOLVED FURTHER, that the President and/or Treasurer of the Corporation undertake all actions as are necessary to administer and implement said plan.

The undersigned hereby certifies that he/she is the duly elected and qualified Secretary and the custodian of the books and records and seal of _____ ,
a corporation duly formed pursuant to the laws of the State of _____ ,
and that the foregoing is a true record of a resolution duly adopted at a meeting of the Board of Directors, and that said meeting was held in accordance with state law and the Bylaws of the above-named Corporation on _____ , 19 ____ , and that said resolution is now in full force and effect without modification or rescission.

IN WITNESS WHEREOF, I have executed my name as Secretary and have hereunto affixed the corporate seal of the above-named Corporation this ____ day of _____ ,
19 ____ .

A True Record.

Attest.

_____
Secretary

RESOLUTION:
AUTHORIZE LEAVE OF ABSENCE

WHEREAS,   has been employed by the

Corporation since   and now requests a personal leave of absence; be

it

RESOLVED, that   is hereby granted a leave of

absence from the Corporation for the period from   , 19   , to

, 19   . Compensation and continuity of fringe benefits during this

absence shall be as provided in the annexed letter authorizing said leave.

The undersigned hereby certifies that he/she is the duly elected and qualified Secretary

and the custodian of the books and records and seal of   ,

a corporation duly formed pursuant to the laws of the State of   ,

and that the foregoing is a true record of a resolution duly adopted at a meeting of the

Board of Directors, and that said meeting was held in accordance with state law and the

Bylaws of the above-named Corporation on   , 19   , and that said

resolution is now in full force and effect without modification or rescission.

IN WITNESS WHEREOF, I have executed my name as Secretary and have hereunto

affixed the corporate seal of the above-named Corporation this   day of   ,

19   .

A True Record.

Attest.

_____
Secretary

RESOLUTION:
AUTHORIZE RAISE

WHEREAS,   as   of

the Corporation currently earns $ per year as a salary, and

WHEREAS, the Corporation wishes to recognize said individual's performance and

contributions to the Corporation by granting a raise; be it

RESOLVED, that the present salary of $ per annum be raised to $

per annum, effective as of   , 19   .

The undersigned hereby certifies that he/she is the duly elected and qualified Secretary

and the custodian of the books and records and seal of   ,

a corporation duly formed pursuant to the laws of the State of   ,

and that the foregoing is a true record of a resolution duly adopted at a meeting of the

Board of Directors, and that said meeting was held in accordance with state law and the

Bylaws of the above-named Corporation on   , 19   , and that said

resolution is now in full force and effect without modification or rescission.

IN WITNESS WHEREOF, I have executed my name as Secretary and have hereunto

affixed the corporate seal of the above-named Corporation this   day of   ,

19   .

A True Record.

Attest.

_____
Secretary

RESOLUTION:
FIX SALARY

RESOLVED, that the salary of the   of the Corporation be fixed at

$ per annum, until further action by the board.

The undersigned hereby certifies that he/she is the duly elected and qualified Secretary

and the custodian of the books and records and seal of   /

a corporation duly formed pursuant to the laws of the State of   /

and that the foregoing is a true record of a resolution duly adopted at a meeting of the

Board of Directors, and that said meeting was held in accordance with state law and the

Bylaws of the above-named Corporation on   , 19   , and that said

resolution is now in full force and effect without modification or rescission.

IN WITNESS WHEREOF, I have executed my name as Secretary and have hereunto

affixed the corporate seal of the above-named Corporation this   day of   /

19   .

A True Record.

Attest.

_____
Secretary

RESOLUTION:
MAKE CHARITABLE CONTRIBUTION

WHEREAS, the Board of Directors deems it to be in the best interests of the Corporation

to make a charitable contribution to   ; be it

RESOLVED, that the Corporation donate to

the generally described assets of the Corporation as:

                                                            ; and be it

RESOLVED FURTHER, that the President and/or Treasurer obtain from counsel an

opinion that said contribution qualifies as a(n)   expense pursuant to

Internal Revenue Service regulations.

The undersigned hereby certifies that he/she is the duly elected and qualified Secretary

and the custodian of the books and records and seal of   ,

a corporation duly formed pursuant to the laws of the State of   ,

and that the foregoing is a true record of a resolution duly adopted at a meeting of the

Board of Directors, and that said meeting was held in accordance with state law and the

Bylaws of the above-named Corporation on   , 19   , and that said

resolution is now in full force and effect without modification or rescission.

IN WITNESS WHEREOF, I have executed my name as Secretary and have hereunto

affixed the corporate seal of the above-named Corporation this   day of   ,

19   .

A True Record.

Attest.

_____
Secretary

RESOLUTION:
MODIFY OFFICER SALARIES

RESOLVED, that the salaries of the officers of the Corporation be adjusted as follows, effective immediately:

President from $_____   to $_____

Vice President from $_____   to $_____

Treasurer from $_____   to $_____

Secretary from $_____   to $_____

And that said salaries remain in force until further action by this board.

The undersigned hereby certifies that he/she is the duly elected and qualified Secretary and the custodian of the books and records and seal of   ,
a corporation duly formed pursuant to the laws of the State of   ,
and that the foregoing is a true record of a resolution duly adopted at a meeting of the Board of Directors, and that said meeting was held in accordance with state law and the Bylaws of the above-named Corporation on   , 19   , and that said resolution is now in full force and effect without modification or rescission.

IN WITNESS WHEREOF, I have executed my name as Secretary and have hereunto affixed the corporate seal of the above-named Corporation this   day of   , 19   .

A True Record.

Attest.

_____
Secretary

RESOLUTION:
PAY OFFICER BONUSES

WHEREAS,   presented to this board recommendations for bonuses to officers, as follows:

To _____, President, $ _____

To _____, Vice President, $ _____

To _____, Secretary, $ _____

To _____, Treasurer, $ _____

RESOLVED, that the said recommendations are hereby approved and adopted, and that the Treasurer of this Corporation is hereby authorized and directed to make payments to the respective officers, in accordance with the above recommendations.

The undersigned hereby certifies that he/she is the duly elected and qualified Secretary and the custodian of the books and records and seal of   , a corporation duly formed pursuant to the laws of the State of   , and that the foregoing is a true record of a resolution duly adopted at a meeting of the Board of Directors, and that said meeting was held in accordance with state law and the Bylaws of the above-named Corporation on   , 19   , and that said resolution is now in full force and effect without modification or rescission.

IN WITNESS WHEREOF, I have executed my name as Secretary and have hereunto affixed the corporate seal of the above-named Corporation this   day of   , 19   .

A True Record.

Attest.

_____
Secretary

RESOLUTION:
REPAY EXCESS COMPENSATION

RESOLVED, that each officer of the Corporation shall be responsible to repay to the Corporation any amount paid to such officer as salary that has been disallowed by the Internal Revenue Service as excess salary or compensation.

The undersigned hereby certifies that he/she is the duly elected and qualified Secretary and the custodian of the books and records and seal of   ,
a corporation duly formed pursuant to the laws of the State of   ,
and that the foregoing is a true record of a resolution duly adopted at a meeting of the Board of Directors, and that said meeting was held in accordance with state law and the Bylaws of the above-named Corporation on   , 19   , and that said resolution is now in full force and effect without modification or rescission.

IN WITNESS WHEREOF, I have executed my name as Secretary and have hereunto affixed the corporate seal of the above-named Corporation this   day of   ,
19   .

A True Record.

Attest.

_____
Secretary

RESOLUTION:
STOCK BONUS FOR OFFICERS

RESOLVED, that as additional compensation and bonus for their services to

_____, 19___, there shall be issued to the following officers of

the company the number of shares of common stock of this Corporation as set opposite

their respective names:

Officer	Position	Number of Shares
_____	_____	_____
_____	_____	_____
_____	_____	_____
_____	_____	_____

The undersigned hereby certifies that he/she is the duly elected and qualified Secretary

and the custodian of the books and records and seal of _____,

a corporation duly formed pursuant to the laws of the State of _____,

and that the foregoing is a true record of a resolution duly adopted at a meeting of the

Board of Directors, and that said meeting was held in accordance with state law and the

Bylaws of the above-named Corporation on _____, 19___, and that said

resolution is now in full force and effect without modification or rescission.

IN WITNESS WHEREOF, I have executed my name as Secretary and have hereunto

affixed the corporate seal of the above-named Corporation this ____ day of _____,

19___ .

A True Record.

Attest.

_____
Secretary

RESOLUTION:
TERMINATE OFFICER SALARIES

RESOLVED, that the salaries of the President, Vice President, Secretary and Treasurer of this Corporation, as fixed by resolution of the Board of Directors at a meeting held on

, 19   , shall be terminated as of   , 19   ; that the said officers shall serve the Corporation as such officers without compensation; and that no salaries shall be paid to the said officers until authorized by the Board of Directors.

The undersigned hereby certifies that he/she is the duly elected and qualified Secretary and the custodian of the books and records and seal of   ,

a corporation duly formed pursuant to the laws of the State of   ,

and that the foregoing is a true record of a resolution duly adopted at a meeting of the Board of Directors, and that said meeting was held in accordance with state law and the Bylaws of the above-named Corporation on   , 19   , and that said resolution is now in full force and effect without modification or rescission.

IN WITNESS WHEREOF, I have executed my name as Secretary and have hereunto affixed the corporate seal of the above-named Corporation this   day of   ,

19   .

A True Record.

Attest.

_____
Secretary

DEPARTMENTS
OF
INCORPORATION

BY STATE

**Every state provides its own specific
Certificate (or Articles) of Incorporation.
Refer to the following pages to find the appropriate address
and phone number for the state in which you will incorporate.**

ALABAMA
Secretary of State
State Capital-Corporations Divisions
P.O. Box 5616
Montgomery, AL 36103-5616
(205)242-5324

ALASKA
State of Alaska
Department of Commerce and
Economic Development
Corporation
Juneau, AK 99811
(907)465-2530

ARIZONA
Arizona Corporation Commission
Incorporating Division
1300 W. Washington Street
Phoenix, AZ 85007
(602)542-3026

ARKANSAS
Secretary of State
State Capitol-Corporations Divisions
Little Rock, AR 72201-1094
(501)682-1010

CALIFORNIA
Secretary of State
1230 J Street
Sacramento, CA 95814
(916)445-0620

COLORADO
Secretary of State
1575 Sherman Street, 2nd Floor
Denver, CO 80203
(303)894-2251

CONNECTICUT
Office of the Secretary of State
State of Connecticut-Corporations Division
30 Trinity Street
Hartford, CT 06106
(203)566-8570

DELAWARE
State of Delaware
Department of State, Division of Incorporation
Townsend Building
P.O. Box 898
Dover, DE 19903
(302)739-3073

DISTRICT OF COLUMBIA
Dept. of Consumer Regulatory Affairs
614 "H" Street N.W., Room 407
Washington, DC 20001
(202)727-7278

FLORIDA
Division of Incorporation
P.O. Box 6327
Tallahassee, FL 32314
(904)488-9000

GEORGIA
Secretary of State
Corporations Department
2 Martin Luther King Drive
Suite 315, West Tower
Atlanta, GA 30334
(404)656-2817

HAWAII
Director of the Dept. of Regulatory Agencies
State Capital
Honolulu, HA 96813
(808)586-2727

IDAHO
Secretary of State
State House, Room 203
Boise, ID 83720
(208)334-2300

ILLINOIS
Secretary of State Dept. of Corporations
328 Howlett Building
Springfield, IL 62756
(217)782-7880

INDIANA
Secretary of State
302 W. Washington St., Room E018
Indianapolis, IN 46204
(317)232-6576

IOWA
Secretary of State
State Capitol
Des Moines, IA 50319
(515)281-5204

KANSAS
State of Kansas
Department of Incorporation
1500 S.W. Arrowhead Drive
Topeka, KS 66604-4027
(913)296-4564

KENTUCKY
Secretary of State
P.O. Box 718
Frankfort, KY 40602-0718
(502)564-2848

LOUISIANA
Secretary of State
P.O. Box 94125
Baton Rouge, LA 70804-9125
(504)925-4704

MAINE
Secretary of State Department of Incorporation
State House, Station 101
Augusta, ME 04333-0101
(207)289-4195

MARYLAND
State Dept. of Assessments and Taxation
301 W. Preston St., Room 809
Baltimore, MD 21201
(410)225-1350

MASSACHUSETTS
Secretary of State
Corporations Division
1 Ashburton Place, 17th Floor
Boston, MA 02108
(6617)727-9640

MICHIGAN
State of Michigan
Department of Commerce
Corporation Division
P.O. Box 30054
Lansing, MI 48909
(517)334-6302

MINNESOTA
Secretary of State
180 State Office Building
St. Paul, MN 55155
(612)296-2803

MISSISSIPPI
Secretary of State
Office of Incorporation
P.O. Box 136
Jackson, MS 39205
(601)359-1633

MISSOURI
Secretary of State
Jefferson City, MO 65101
(314)751-4153

MONTANA
Secretary of State
Capitol Bldg., Room 225
Helena, MT 59620
(406)444-2034

NEBRASKA
Secretary of State-Corporate Division
Suite 1301, Capitol Bldg.
Lincoln, NE 68509
(402)471-4079

NEVADA
Secretary of State-Capital Complex
Carson City, NV 89710
(702)687-5203

NEW HAMPSHIRE
Department of Revenue Administration
Return Processing Division
P.O. Box 637
Concord, NH 03301
(603)271-3246

NEW JERSEY
State of New Jersey
Department of State
P.O. Box 1330
Trenton, NJ 08625
(609)530-6400

NEW MEXICO
State Corporation Commission
Franchise Tax Department
P.O. Drawer 1269
Santa Fe, NM 87504-1269
(505)827-4504

NEW YORK
State of New York
Department of State
Division of Corporations
162 Washington Avenue
Albany, NY 12231
(518)473-2492

NORTH CAROLINA
Secretary of State
Raleigh, NC 27603
(919)733-4201

NORTH DAKOTA
Secretary of State
Bismark, ND 58505
(701)224-4284

OHIO
Secretary of State
30 East Broad Street, 14th Floor
Columbus, OH 43266-0418
(614)466-3910

OKLAHOMA
Secretary of State
101 State Capitol
Oklahoma City, OK 73105
(405)521-3911

OREGON
Department of Commerce
Corporation Division
158 12th street N.E.
Salem, OR 97310
(503)378-4166

PENNSYLVANIA
Commonwealth of Pennsylvania
Corporations Office
Department of Sate
301 N. Office Bldg.
Harrisburg, PA 17120
(717)787-1057

PUERTO RICO
Commonwealth of Puerto Rico
Department of State
P.O. Box 3271
San Juan, PR 00902-3271
(809)722-2121

RHODE ISLAND
Secretary of State – Dept. of Corporations
100 N. Main Street
Providence, RI 02903
(401)277-3040

SOUTH CAROLINA
P.O. Box 11350
Columbia, SC 29211
(803)734-2158

SOUTH DAKOTA
Secretary of State-Attn. Corporations
500 E. Capitol
Pierre, SD 57501
(605)773-4845

TENNESSEE
Department of State
Division of Services, Suite 1800
James K. Polk Building
Nashville, TN 37243-0306
(615)741-2286

TEXAS
Secretary of State
Austin, TX 78711
(512)463-5555

UTAH
Department of Commerce
Heber M.Wells Building
160 E. 300 South, 2nd Floor
Salt Lake City, UT 84111
(801)530-4849

VERMONT
Secretary of State-Corporations Division
109 State Street
Montpelier, VT 05609-1104
(802)828-2386

VIRGINIA
Commonwealth of Virginia
State Corporation Commission
P.O. Box 1197
Richmond, VA 23209
(804)371-9967

WASHINGTON
Secretary of State – Corporation Division
Olympia, WA 98504
(206)753-7115

WEST VIRGINIA
Secretary of State's Office
State Capitol
Charleston, WV 25305
(304) 558-8000

WISCONSIN
Secretary of State
P.O. Box 7846
Madison, WI 53707
(608)266-3590

WYOMING
Secretary of State-Corporations Division
State Capitol Bldg.
Cheyenne, WY 82002
(307)777-7311

Glossary of Useful Terms

Assets—Anything owned with monetary value. This includes both real and personal property.

Authorized shares—The number of shares a corporation is authorized to sell.

Bylaws—Rules adopted by the corporation itself for the regulation of a corporation's own actions; a subordinate law adopted by a corporation, association, or other body for its self-government or to regulate the rights and duties of its officers and members.

C corporation—A regular corporation that is not an S corporation.

Calendar year—The accounting year beginning on January 1 and ending on December 31.

Certificate or Articles of Incorporation—The document that creates a corporation according to the laws of the state. This must be filed and approved by the state.

Consolidation—When two corporations combine, creating a third.

Deceptively similar—A name so similar to another name that the two become confused in the public eye.

Dividend income—Dividends that must be declared as regular income for income tax purposes

Fiscal year—Any 12-month period used by a business as its fiscal accounting period. Such accounting period may, for example, run from July 1 of one year through June 30 of the next year.

Foreign corporation—A corporation formed in one state or country but conducting some or all of its business in another state or country.

Incorporate—To form a corporation or to organize and be granted status as a corporation by following procedures prescribed by law.

Incorporator—The person who signs the Articles of Incorporation upon petitioning the state for a corporate charter.

Insolvency—Bankruptcy.

Issued shares—The number of shares actually sold by the corporation.

Merger—The absorption of one corporation by another.

Minority stockholder—One who owns or controls less than 50 percent of the stock in a corporation.

Minutes—Written records of formal proceedings of stockholders' and directors' meetings.

Non-par value stock—Shares of stock without specified value.

Not-for-profit corporation—A corporation organized for some charitable, civil, social or other purpose that does not entail the generation of profit or the distribution of its income to members, principals, shareholders, officers or others affiliated with it. Such corporations are accorded special treatment under the law for some purposes, including taxation.

Parliamentary procedure—Rules such as "Roberts Rules of Order," which govern stockholders' meetings, directors' meetings, etc.

Par value stock—Shares of stock with a specified value.

Proxy—Authorization by a stockholder allowing another to vote his shares of stock.

Publicly owned corporation—One whose stock is owned by more than 25 stockholders and is regulated by the Securities and Exchange Commission.

Quorum—A majority of the stockholders or directors necessary for vote-counting and decision-making at a meeting. While a quorum is usually a majority of either the total membership or the members present, a quorum may consist of a greater number than a simple majority if desired and stated in the bylaws.

Regular corporation—Also known as a C Corporation.

Service business—A business that sells service or advice instead of a tangible product.

Shareholder—See Stockholder.

Start-up venture—A new business having no track record.

State statutes—Laws created by a state legislature.

Statutory agent—A lawyer, corporation or individual who has assumed the responsibility of being the legal representative for the corporation for purposes of accepting legal service in a certain state.

S Corporation (Subchapter S Corporation)—A small business corporation which elects to be taxed as a partnership or proprietorship for federal income tax purposes. Individual shareholders enjoy the benefits under state law of limited corporate liability, but avoid corporate federal taxes.

Stock certificate—Written instrument evidencing a share in the ownership of a corporation.

Stockholder—A holder of one or more shares of the stock of a corporation. A stockholder may be called a "shareholder."

Subsidiary—A corporation owned by another corporation.

E·Z Legal® Software

☑ Check out the
E·Z LEGAL® LIBRARY

Valid in all 50 states

☑ GUIDES

Each comprehensive guide contains the valid forms, samples, instructions, information and suggestions you need to proceed.

Plus state-by-state requirements, a handy glossary and the valuable 10-page supplement "How to Save on Attorney Fees."

☑ KITS

Each kit includes a clear, concise instruction manual to help you understand your rights and obligations, plus the ready-to-complete forms you need.

For the busy do-it-yourselfer, it's quick, it's affordable, it's E-Z.

GUIDES	KITS	TITLES
✔	✔	**Bankruptcy** Take the confusion out of filing bankruptcy.
✖	✖	**Buying/Selling a Home** Learn the ins and outs on moving in or out.
✖	✖	**Collecting Child Support** Ensure your kids the support they deserve.
✔	✔	**Credit Repair** It's got all the tools to put you back on track.
✔	✔	**Divorce** Learn to proceed on your own, without a lawyer.
✔	✖	**Employment Law** A handy reference for employers and employees.
✔	✖	**Immigration** A must-have for immigrants and aliens.
✔	✔	**Incorporation** Find all the forms to get your company INC'ed.
✔	✔	**Last Will & Testament** Write a will the right way, the E-Z way.
✔	✔	**Living Will & P.O.A.** Take steps now to ensure Death with Dignity.
✔	✔	**Living Trust** Trust us to help you provide for your loved ones.
✔	✔	**Small Claims Court** Prepare for court... or explore other avenues.
✔	✖	**Trademarks & Copyrights** Leave your mark, have your rights to it protected.
✔	✔	**Traffic Court** Learn your rights on the road and in court.

✖ – Fall '96 Release

LEGAL LIBRARY CARD

E·Z LEGAL FORMS®

... when you need it in writing!®

Valid at:

Super Stores, Office Supply Stores, Drug Stores, Hardware Stores, Bookstores and other fine retailers.

ss E-Z gids/kits